Overcoming the Trauma
of Your Motor Vehicle Accident

Overcoming the Trauma of Your Motor Vehicle Accident

A COGNITIVE-BEHAVIORAL TREATMENT PROGRAM

Therapist Guide

Edward J. Hickling • Edward B. Blanchard

OXFORD
UNIVERSITY PRESS

2006

OXFORD

UNIVERSITY PRESS

Oxford University Press, Inc., publishes works that further
Oxford University's objective of excellence
in research, scholarship, and education.

Oxford   New York
Auckland   Cape Town   Dar es Salaam   Hong Kong   Karachi
Kuala Lumpur   Madrid   Melbourne   Mexico City   Nairobi
New Delhi   Shanghai   Taipei   Toronto

With offices in
Argentina   Austria   Brazil   Chile   Czech Republic   France   Greece
Guatemala   Hungary   Italy   Japan   Poland   Portugal   Singapore
South Korea   Switzerland   Thailand   Turkey   Ukraine   Vietnam

Published by Oxford University Press, Inc.
198 Madison Avenue, New York, New York 10016

www.oup.com

Oxford is a registered trademark of Oxford University Press

Library of Congress Cataloging-in-Publication Data
Hickling, Edward J.
Overcoming the trauma of your motor vehicle accident :
a cognitive-behavioral treatment program, therapist guide /
Edward J. Hickling, Edward B. Blanchard.
      p. cm.—(Treatments that work)
   Includes bibliographical references.
   ISBN-13 978-0-19-530605-7; 978-0-19-530606-4 (pbk.)
   ISBN 0-19-530605-8; 0-19-530606-6 (pbk.)
      1. Traffic accident victims—Rehabilitation—Problems, exercises, etc.
      2. Cognitive therapy—Problems, exercises, etc.   3. Traffic
      accidents—Psychological aspects.   I. Blanchard, Edward B.   II. Title.
      III. Series.
   RC1045.P78H532 2006
   616.89′142—dc22   2006000898

9 8 7 6 5 4 3 2 1

Printed in the United States of America
on acid-free paper

About Treatments That Work™

Stunning developments in health care have taken place over the last several years, but many of the widely accepted interventions and strategies in mental health and behavioral medicine have been brought into question by research evidence as not only lacking benefit, but also perhaps inducing harm. Other strategies have been proven effective using the best current standards of evidence, resulting in broad-based recommendations to make these practices more available to the public. Several recent developments are behind this revolution. First, we have arrived at a much deeper understanding of pathology, both psychological and physical, and this understanding has led to the development of new, more precisely targeted interventions. Second, our research methodologies have improved substantially, such that we have reduced threats to internal and external validity, making the outcomes more directly applicable to clinical situations. Third, governments around the world, as well as health care systems and policymakers, have decided that the quality of care should improve, that it should be evidence-based, and that it is in the public's interest to ensure that this happens (Barlow, 2004; Institute of Medicine, 2001).

Of course, the major stumbling block for clinicians everywhere is the accessibility of newly developed evidence-based psychological interventions. Workshops and books can go only so far in acquainting responsible and conscientious practitioners with the latest behavioral health care practices and their applicability to individual patients. This new series, Treatments That Work™, is devoted to communicating these exciting new interventions to clinicians on the frontline of practice.

The manuals and workbooks in this series contain step-by-step, detailed procedures for assessing and treating patients with specific problems and diagnoses. However, this series also goes beyond the books and manuals by providing ancillary materials that approximate the supervisory process in assisting practitioners in implementing these procedures in practice.

In our emerging health care system, the growing consensus is that evidence-based practice offers the most responsible course of action for the mental health professional. All behavioral health care clinicians deeply desire to provide the best possible care for their patients. In this series, our aim is to close the dissemination and information gap and make that possible.

This therapist guide and the companion workbook for clients address the treatment of posttraumatic stress disorder due to severe motor vehicle accidents (MVAs) or related events. MVAs are surprisingly common, resulting annually in personal injury in over 3 million victims in the United States alone. However, the physical injuries often have less impact in the long run than the severe emotional distress, flashbacks, and substantial impairment in work or family life. Yet, few people seek treatment immediately, mostly because they are not aware of the nature of their condition or do not realize that successful brief treatments are available.

During the past 15 years, we have developed increasingly effective treatments for PTSD, to the point where these interventions compare favorably to the best psychological treatments for other disorders (Keane & Barlow, 2002). These treatments also have the advantage of proven durability after treatment ends, with the added benefit of allowing substantial reduction or elimination of any medications prescribed prior to this treatment. The approach described in this manual was developed by two of the pioneers in this area, with decades of experience in developing and testing new treatments, and their substantial experience will come through in the case examples and solutions to the many individual issues that arise during the course of treatment. This program is a welcome addition to our growing list of psychological treatments with empirical support, when administered by skilled clinicians.

David H. Barlow, Editor-in-Chief,
Treatments That Work™
Boston, MA

Contents

Overcoming the Trauma
of Your Motor Vehicle Accident

Chapter 1 | *Introductory Information for Therapists*

Case Study: Mary

■ *The day had begun like any other. Mary was on her way to work early in the morning. She had many things on her mind that morning, the morning her accident occurred. The first thing she saw was a huge shadow that came over her; her next memory was the sound of squealing brakes. Then there was a huge impact. Mary awakened in a daze. She was unsure how long she had been lying there. She saw that the contents of her purse had been scattered around the car. Mary's next memory was of someone talking to her. He didn't make sense. She didn't know who he was or why he was there. It was hard to see. She could taste blood dripping into her mouth. The taste of the blood made her sick to her stomach. She remembers hearing someone say, "Are you all right? Are you all right?" She drifted in and out of awareness for a while, and then she heard a police officer say, "Just lie still. We'll have you out of there soon."*

Then it dawned on her. She'd been in a terrible crash, and she was hurt! After that, it was a blur. Mary moved in and out of awareness. She next remembered being at a hospital, with doctors asking a lot of questions and ordering tests. She was scared about what would happen next. All she could think was, "I could have died!" "I didn't do anything wrong!" "How could this have happened to me?" ■

Background Information and Purpose of This Program

This therapist manual accompanies the client workbook *Overcoming the Trauma of Your Motor Vehicle Accident*. The treatment and the manuals are designed for use by a therapist who is familiar with cognitive-behavioral therapy (CBT).

Posttraumatic stress disorder (PTSD) is one of the major consequences of motor vehicle accidents (MVAs) in which personal injury occurs.

Based on the studies to date, we estimate that PTSD occurs in 10% to 45% of survivors of MVAs involving personal injury. The largest study (Ehlers, Mayou, & Bryant, 1998) of about 890 consecutive patients treated in an emergency department after an MVA found that 25% met the criteria for PTSD 3 months after the accident. Given the more than 3 million individuals injured in the United States each year (U.S. National Highway Traffic Safety Administration, 2001), our best estimate is that there are about 750,000 new cases of PTSD following MVAs in the United States alone each year. Follow-up studies (e.g., Blanchard, Hickling, et al. 1996) indicate that about 50% of acute cases of PTSD remit, at least in part, by 5 months after the accident, and a further 16% remit by the 1-year point. The remaining one third of cases (approximately 250,000) become chronic and show very, very gradual improvement over the next 5 to 6 years (Kessler, Sonnega, Bromet, Hughes, & Nelson, 1995).

Even with this widespread prevalence of MVA-associated trauma, psychological assessment and treatment of the survivors of car accidents has not received the attention that it deserved until the last 5 to 10 years. Ongoing research has come largely from a number of research centers in England and Canada, as well as from our group in Albany, the Center for Stress and Anxiety Disorders, and the MVA Research Project.

Diagnostic Criteria for Posttraumatic Stress Disorder

Following are the diagnostic criteria for PTSD, according to the American Psychiatric Association *Diagnostic and Statistical Manual of Mental Disorders,* 4th edition (1994).

A. The person has been exposed to a traumatic event in which both of the following were present:
   (1) The person experienced, witnessed, or was confronted with an event or events that involved actual or threatened death or serious injury, or a threat to the physical integrity of self or others.

(2) The person's response involved intense fear, helplessness, or horror. *Note:* In children, this may be expressed instead by disorganized or agitated behavior.

B. The traumatic event is persistently reexperienced in one (or more) of the following ways:
    (1) Recurrent and intrusive distressing recollections of the event, including images, thoughts, or perceptions. *Note:* In young children, repetitive play may occur in which themes or aspects of the trauma are expressed.
    (2) Recurrent distressing dreams of the event. *Note:* In children, there may be frightening dreams without recognizable content.
    (3) Acting or feeling as if the traumatic event were recurring (includes a sense of reliving the experience, illusions, hallucinations, and dissociative flashback episodes, including those that occur upon awakening or when intoxicated). *Note:* In young children, trauma-specific reenactment may occur.
    (4) Intense psychological distress at exposure to internal or external cures that symbolize or resemble an aspect of the traumatic event.
    (5) Physiological reactivity on exposure to internal or external cues that symbolize or resemble an aspect of the traumatic event.

C. Persistent avoidance of stimuli associated with the trauma and numbing of general responsiveness (not present before the trauma), as indicated by three (or more) of the following:
    (1) Efforts to avoid thoughts, feelings, or conversations associated with the trauma
    (2) Efforts to avoid activities, places, or people that arouse recollections of the trauma
    (3) Inability to recall an important aspect of the trauma
    (4) Markedly diminished interest or participation in significant activities
    (5) Feeling of detachment or estrangement from others
    (6) Restricted range of affect (e.g., unable to have loving feelings)
    (7) Sense of foreshortened future (e.g., does not expect to have a career, marriage, children, or a normal life span)

D. Persistent symptoms of increased arousal (not present before the trauma), as indicated by two (or more) of the following:
  (1) Difficulty falling or staying asleep
  (2) Irritability or outbursts of anger
  (3) Difficulty concentrating
  (4) Hypervigilance
  (5) Exaggerated startle response

E. Duration of the disturbance (symptoms in Criteria B, C, and D) is more than 1 month.

F. The disturbance causes clinically significant distress or impairment in social, occupational, or other important areas of functioning.

Specify if:

Acute: if duration of symptoms is less than 3 months.

Chronic: if duration of symptoms is 3 months or more.

Specify if:

With delayed onset: if onset of symptoms is at least 6 months after the stressor.

Development of This Treatment Program

This CBT program was developed over several years as an ancillary part of our initial descriptive follow-up studies of individuals who had been involved in MVAs. That descriptive research was summarized in Blanchard and Hickling (2004).

Our first step was to review the records of clients in our follow-up study who had been treated by two therapists (including the first author, EJH) as part of the clinical responsibility to the participants. The techniques and procedures used were retrieved from clinician records, and assessment data were obtained from the research records. Over an average of 10.5 sessions, there was a 47% decrease in scores, as measured on a structured interview to assess PTSD.

Next, we created a 10-session structured treatment plan that primarily consisted of CBT. Each of the authors used this treatment with a new sample of 10 MVA survivors. This uncontrolled trial (Hickling & Blanchard, 1997) revealed a 67% reduction in PTSD symptom scores at the end of treatment, which improved to 73% at 3-month follow-up. Nine of the 10 clients were improved in terms of diagnosis.

Finally, we (Hickling & Blanchard, 1999) tested our supportive psychotherapy treatment on a new sample of eight clients who had been involved in an MVA. This treatment led to a 46% reduction in PTSD symptom scores.

With the final piece of pilot work completed, we were ready for our National Institute of Mental Health–sponsored randomized controlled trial comparing 10 sessions (flexibly applied to 8–12 sessions) of structured treatment, 10 sessions of supportive psychotherapy, and an assessment/wait list control condition.

This program was developed at the Center for Stress and Anxiety Disorders at the State University of New York, Albany, over the past 15 years. The initial idea for the investigation of PTSD after MVAs came from clients seen in clinical practice. The initial investigations were concerned with psychological disorders that follow car crashes and why some people seem to do quite well following this trauma, while others have significant problems.

The treatment program was a natural evolution of the assessment studies. Initial investigations were case studies that applied CBT approaches to PTSD for this population. Once we found a combination of interventions that targeted each symptom cluster of PTSD, we were able to win additional grant support to conduct empirical studies looking at the clinical effectiveness of these interventions. This treatment proved very successful when applied in a flexible, manual-based format (Blanchard & Hickling, 2004).

Over 15 years of working with MVA survivors, we have continued to look for greater flexibility and application of our treatment. One goal was to share our treatment approach with skilled clinicians who could benefit from the knowledge gained for this trauma population.

The treatment program, in addition to attending to the PTSD that can often follow a car crash, addresses travel anxiety, which is a fairly common problem for most survivors of an MVA. Additionally, other anxiety disorders and even mood disorders have been found to improve in many individuals after the manual-based treatment. Additional issues, such as anger management, existential concerns about the meaning of life, and facing one's mortality, are also common problems that have been included as part of the treatment approach.

Research on This Treatment Program

Assessment Studies

Our own research (Blanchard & Hickling, 1997, 2004) initially focused on individuals who were physically injured in their accidents and sought medical attention. We considered these clients survivors of serious MVAs. In this way, we excluded individuals who had smaller, "fender bender" accidents, although we understand that they, too, can have noticeable psychological effects. In our research efforts, we wanted to focus on individuals who would most likely be seen in a doctor's office.

The Albany MVA Project studied a large number of individuals who had PTSD after an MVA. The first study followed individuals who had PTSD 1 to 4 months after the MVA. The second study followed them up to 1 year after their accident, and some were followed even longer. These individuals did not receive psychological treatment, and they represent what we believe is the natural history of recovery following an MVA.

By the 6-month follow-up point, 55% of the clients studied showed some remission of symptoms. More than half showed full recovery, while the remaining survivors with PTSD showed some improvement. In contrast, 45% showed no change in symptoms, retaining the diagnosis of PTSD over the first 6-month period.

The second study looked at the results of 1-year follow-up of the MVA survivors. After the first 6 months, the degree of remission had essentially begun to plateau, with only 16% showing some remission by the

1-year point. Then, over the next year, there was very little additional change. The number of people who still met the full criteria for PTSD stayed at about 30%.

Our findings showed that the majority of MVA survivors who have acute PTSD show noticeable, spontaneous improvement over the first 6 to 8 months. Approximately one third show complete recovery with no intervention. Thereafter, there is very gradual remission, with about 65% showing some improvement at 12 months. Other researchers have noted continued, gradual improvement as far as 6 years post-trauma in their retrospective study of a large sample of mixed trauma survivors with PTSD (i.e., survivors of trauma other than exclusively MVAs).

It is important to remember that improvement in PTSD symptoms is not the same as absence of symptoms. In these clients, improvement means that the symptoms decreased, not that they disappeared totally.

Treatment Studies

Our treatment study looked at 78 MVA survivors who had chronic PTSD at least 6 months after their accident. They were divided into three groups. Those in the first group received CBT, those in the second group received supportive psychotherapy, and those in the third group were assessed over time as part of a wait list control group. Those who received CBT showed the greatest improvement, with 76.2% no longer meeting the diagnostic criteria for PTSD, as compared with only 47.6% in the supportive treatment group, and 23.8% in the wait list control group. In the CBT group, 82% of participants showed a reduction in the symptoms of major depression versus only 28% in the supportive psychotherapy group and 30% in the wait list control group. Similar results were found for generalized anxiety disorder, with 75% of the CBT group showing improvement versus 18% and 37% in the supportive psychotherapy group and the wait list control group, respectively.

At 1-year follow-up, our data showed that there continued to be a statistically significant advantage of CBT on a categorical diagnosis (PTSD or not) and on the Clinician Administered PTSD Scale (CAPS) scores compared with the group that received supportive psychotherapy. At

2-year follow-up, while there continued to be arithmetic differences favoring CBT treatment for PTSD over supportive psychotherapy, significant differences were found only for the scores on the PTSD Checklist (PCL)and the Impact of Events Scale.

Comorbidity

In addition to PTSD, there is a high likelihood that injured MVA survivors will have two comorbid conditions: travel anxiety and major depressive disorder. We believe that there should be initial and ongoing assessment of these two conditions during treatment.

The good news from our research (Blanchard, Hickling, Devineni, Veazey, Galovski, Mundy, et al., 2003) is that there is a high likelihood of improvement of major depression and travel anxiety with our CBT program for PTSD.

Travel Anxiety

It is very common for individuals to have difficulty with travel behavior after an MVA. Between 72% and 93% of those who have been in a serious MVA will have psychological difficulty when they are either a passenger or a driver in an automobile following their MVA.

Depression

Clinical depression is a common comorbid condition that frequently accompanies PTSD or Acute Stress Disorder (ASD) following an MVA. About 53% of the people in our study who had PTSD also had major depression.

Outline of the Treatment Program

For treatment purposes, we divided the 17 symptoms of PTSD into four clusters, rather than the three imposed by the DSM-IV classification. Then we introduced treatment techniques to target each of the clusters. In fact, several factor analytic studies have supported the four-factor structure for PTSD. The clusters are as follows:

- Reexperiencing the trauma

- Avoidance

- Numbing and estrangement

- Hyperarousal

As a rough approximation, we use the CBT techniques indicated in table 1.1 to counter the symptoms of PTSD as shown.

Table 1.2 shows an outline of the components of treatment.

The treatment program is described in this manual and in the workbook for *Overcoming the Trauma of Your Motor Vehicle Accident* as a 10-session program. For some clients, seven or eight sessions may be enough. In our controlled research, we used a flexible, manual-based approach that included 8 to 12 sessions, based on therapist judgment. Overall, the controlled research had a mean of 10 sessions. (We also had a number of participants who had made progress in 12 sessions, but who needed more treatment to achieve a higher level of functioning). You, as the therapist, will need to use your clinical experience and judgment, which is aided by the ongoing structured reassessments provided as a part of this treat-

Table 1.1 How Treatment Techniques Target PTSD Symptom Clusters

Technique	Targeted Symptom Cluster
Relaxation training	Hyperarousal
Writing and reading an MVA description	Reexperiencing and avoidance
Graduated imaginal and in vivo exposure	Avoidance and reexperiencing
Cognitive therapy techniques	Avoidance (to help cope with arousal from exposure and anxiety from intrusive memories)
Pleasant Events scheduling	Numbing and estrangement
Psychoeducation about MVAs and PTSD	All clusters

Table 1.2 Treatment Components and Timeline

	Week 1	Week 2	Week 3	Week 4	Week 5	Week 6	Weeks 7–9	Week 10
Intervention	Provide psychoeducation, practice relaxation, write an MVA description (week 1), meet with the spouse or partner							
		Rate travel situations with SUDS; read the MVA description three to four times per day; practice 11-, 8-, and 4-muscle-group relaxation exercises; begin or use coping self-statements; build and apply the travel hierarchy (use as needed)						
				Begin cognitive reappraisal, continue the relaxation exercises, practice relaxation, introduce relaxation-by-recall, continue to read the MVA description, begin and continue imaginal and in vivo exposure to the travel hierarchy, continue with coping statements				
						Review all skills or tools learned up to this point; explore issues of mortality, anger, depression, or isolation (as needed)		
	Entire treatment typically takes 8 to 12 weeks							

ment, to determine when your client has achieved the treatment goals. An outline of the treatment sessions follows. (It is assumed, at this point, that you have met with the client at least once, agreed on the diagnosis, and either had the client purchase the workbook, or given the client the assessment forms to complete before the initial meeting for treatment).

Session 1. Provide psychoeducation. Review the client self-assessment from the PTSD Checklist for the symptoms of PTSD. Explain that PTSD is a normal reaction to abnormal circumstances. Describe symptom clusters and the techniques that will be used to help. Begin relaxation training. Assign a written description of the client's MVA as homework.

Session 2. Review the homework. Review the client's understanding of PTSD (avoidance or continuation of anxiety, as well as the need for exposure-based intervention). Review the client's written description of the MVA, and incorporate it into the next homework assignment. Continue relaxation training. Arrange a time to meet with the client's spouse or partner, if possible.

Session 3. Review the homework. Have the client read their MVA description aloud. Discuss negative self-talk. Begin work on mastery and coping self-statements. Meet with the client's spouse or partner, if scheduled. Continue relaxation training. Introduce travel hierarchy.

Session 4. Review the homework. Introduce cognitive reappraisal. Discuss the driving hierarchy. Continue relaxation training.

Session 5. Review the homework. Introduce relaxation-by-recall. Discuss driving, cognitive techniques and their application, imaginal exposure as needed, and in vivo exposure. Ask the client to complete assessment instruments as a midtreatment measure.

Session 6. Review the homework. Introduce cue-conditioned relaxation. Continue working with CBT and the exposure model.

Session 7. Review the homework. Introduce numbing, pleasant event scheduling, existential concerns, anger, and depression and isolation.

Session 8. Review the homework. Flexibly apply interventions, as indicated.

Session 9. Review the homework. Flexibly apply interventions, as indicated.

Session 10. Review the homework. This is the termination session, unless the decision has been made to continue treatment. Review the reassessment instruments and treatment interventions.

Sessions are based on a 50- to 60-minute treatment period. On some occasions, you may need to adjust the content of the session and the rate at which you present the material, depending on how rapidly or slowly the client is able to use or understand the material. Typically, sessions begin with a review of the homework assigned the week before. This will allow the therapist to make a decision about how ready the client is for the next step in treatment. During most of the sessions, new material is introduced in a planned fashion. As much as possible, the client should be engaged in a dialogue to make sure that he or she grasps the material and is able to use it in the fashion desired.

The first six sessions are typically fairly structured to ensure that material is presented that addresses the core symptoms of PTSD after an MVA. The remaining sessions are then approached more flexibly, to address the individual needs of each client with PTSD as he or she is adjusting to the aftermath of a traumatic crash. Therefore, with some clients, it may be necessary to spend additional time on issues of numbing, estrangement, anger, or mortality.

The use of assessment tools that address the symptoms of PTSD, depression, and travel anxiety is considered an integral part of the treatment. These tools allow the client and the therapist to stay focused on the symptoms of PTSD and to discuss the improvements or lack of improvements in a timely and targeted fashion.

Chapter 2 | *Client Self-Assessment*

Assessment of Post–Motor Vehicle Accident Distress (or How Do I Know How I'm Doing?)

Some of the questions that many people have after an accident include, "How am I doing?" and "Are the things I'm feeling normal, or do I need help?"

Chapters 3, 9, and 12 of the workbook provide clients with a number of questionnaires and tests that will help them to see how they are doing emotionally.

The first questionnaire provided for the client is the PTSD Checklist (PCL), which is used to assess the symptoms of PTSD. The second questionnaire is the Travel Anxiety Questionnaire (TAQ), which assesses travel anxiety and driving phobia. The third assessment provided is the depression scale developed by the Center for Epidemiologic Studies (CES-D).

In the workbook, we ask the client to complete these assessments at various stages throughout the treatment. The client should complete the assessments before the initial session, after session 5, and before the final session (usually session 10). Although these are self-assessments, it is imperative to stress to the client that these questionnaires are not a substitute for meeting with a qualified mental health professional for the assessment and diagnosis of a disorder. The questionnaires are not provided for that purpose. They are meant to be a "psychological yardstick" to help clients measure how they are doing and to provide a reference point with which they can compare their scores with those of other people who have also gone through an MVA trauma.

As the therapist, it is your job to assign the task of completing the assessments and to review them in session.

Posttraumatic Stress Disorder Checklist

Below we have provided the case study of Mary, as well as her sample, filled-out PCL.

Case Study: Mary

The day had begun like any other. Mary was on her way to work early in the morning. She had many things on her mind that morning, the morning her accident occurred. The first thing she saw was a huge shadow that came over her; her next memory was the sound of squealing brakes. Then there was a huge impact. Mary awakened in a daze. She was unsure how long she had been lying there. She saw that the contents of her purse had been scattered around the car. Mary's next memory was of someone talking to her. He didn't make sense. She didn't know who he was or why he was there. It was hard to see. She could taste blood dripping into her mouth. The taste of the blood made her sick to her stomach. She remembers hearing someone say, "Are you all right? Are you all right?" She drifted in and out of awareness for a while, and then she heard a police officer say, "Just lie still. We'll have you out of there soon."

Then it dawned on her. She'd been in a terrible crash, and she was hurt! After that, it was a blur. Mary moved in and out of awareness. She next remembered being at a hospital, with doctors asking a lot of questions and ordering tests. She was scared about what would happen next. All she could think was, "I could have died!" "I didn't do anything wrong!" "How could this have happened to me?"

About 2 months after her accident, Mary completed the questionnaire as to how she had been feeling over the past month (figure 2.1). On one item, feeling as if her future would be cut short, she replied "not at all." When her scores are totaled, we find that she had a tally of 8 for items she felt "a little bit," 12 for items she felt "moderately," 24 for items she felt "quite a bit," and 10 for the two items she felt "extremely." This resulted in a total score of 55. This score is above the level that predicts

Figure 2.1 Current Posttraumatic Stress Disorder Checklist (PCL)

Name: _Mary_   Date: _____

Instructions: Following is a list of problems and complaints that people sometimes have in response to stressful life experiences (i.e., your most distressing MVA). Please read each one carefully, and then circle one of the numbers to the right to indicate how much you were bothered by that problem *in the past month*.

	Not at All	A Little Bit	Moderately	Quite a Bit	Extremely
1. Repeated, disturbing memories, thoughts, or images of the stressful experience?	1	2	3	(4)	5
2. Repeated, disturbing dreams of the stressful experience?	1	2	(3)	4	5
3. Suddenly acting or feeling as if the stressful experience were happening again (as if you were reliving it)?	1	(2)	3	4	5
4. Feeling very upset when something reminded you of the stressful experience?	1	2	3	4	(5)
5. Having a physical reaction (e.g., heart pounding, trouble breathing, sweating) when something reminded you of the stressful experience?	1	2	3	(4)	5
6. Avoiding thinking about or talking about your stressful experience or avoiding having feelings related to it?	1	2	(3)	4	5
7. Avoiding activities or situations because they reminded you of your stressful experience?	1	2	3	4	(5)
8. Trouble remembering important parts of the stressful experience?	1	(2)	3	4	5
9. Loss of interest in activities that you used to enjoy?	1	2	3	(4)	5
10. Feeling distant or cut off from others?	1	(2)	3	4	5
11. Feeling emotionally numb or being unable to have loving feelings for those close to you?	1	(2)	3	4	5
12. Feeling as if your future somehow will be cut short?	(1)	2	3	4	5
13. Trouble falling or staying asleep?	1	2	3	(4)	5
14. Feeling irritable or having angry outbursts?	1	2	3	(4)	5
15. Having difficulty concentrating?	1	2	(3)	4	5
16. Being "super-alert," watchful, or on guard?	1	2	3	(4)	5
17. Feeling jumpy or easily startled?	1	2	(3)	4	5
Total	1	8	12	24	10

PTSD (44 or higher), making it likely that she is experiencing PTSD. Her score of 55 is similar to that of the group that is likely to have PTSD 2 years later if left untreated. Mary would benefit from seeking help.

Travel Anxiety Questionnaire

Following is the case study of Paula, as well as her sample, filled-out TAQ.

Case Study: Paula

Paula remembered her first car vividly, a red Mustang convertible. She loved to drive! Paula was always the one who picked up her friends and drove to the beach, the store, or wherever they were going. Then she had her accident. Now, her love of driving is gone. In fact, it's closer to torture for her to get behind the wheel and go anywhere. Yes, she'll drive to work and home afterward. She will drive to the doctor's office and to the store for essentials. But now, she feels scared and anxious. She had once loved to drive! No matter how much she tells herself that her feelings are unreasonable, they don't go away. Some times and places are worse than others. Now, she dreads rush hour and bad weather. When there is rain or snow, Paula experiences near panic or refuses to drive at all. Riding in a car isn't any better, but at least when she's behind the wheel, she knows what she's going to do next.

It is very common for anyone who has been in an MVA to have some anxiety or discomfort when driving. In its worst form, this can result in a panic attack. A panic attack is a very intense period of anxiety that can include symptoms such as heart palpitations or accelerated heart rate, sweating, trembling or shaking, shortness of breath, a feeling of choking, chest pain or discomfort, nausea or stomach distress, dizziness or feeling faint, numbing or tingling sensations in the arms or legs, and hot flashes or chills. Panic attacks can also include feelings of unreality or feeling detached from oneself, fear of losing control or going crazy, and a fear of dying.

Anxiety related to driving can take many forms. It can be a physical sensation that is described as a state of tension or muscular tightness; it can also be a feeling of fear or apprehension that something bad is about to occur. Whatever the feeling, it can affect one's driving.

Driving can be limited in a couple of ways. Some people avoid it outright, simply refusing to drive. This can lead to the need to rely on others to drive or the need to take public transportation in a person who formerly drove himself or herself. Driving can often be avoided. For example, a person may not drive in certain places (e.g., the scene of the accident, major highways, congested roads) or may avoid certain weather or driving conditions (e.g., darkness, unfamiliar places, bad weather). Being a passenger is often even worse than being the driver. At least the driver has some control. A passenger is "out of control" and totally "at the mercy of the driver" and his or her skills and reactions.

The TAQ addresses a number of these concerns in a self-report format. This questionnaire looks at specific areas of driving behavior that may have been negatively affected by the MVA. Although the score of the questionnaire is obtained for both the degree of avoidance and the amount of anxiety experienced, there are no critical levels that indicate the presence or absence of travel anxiety. For some items (e.g., driving in snow), the answers are dependent on where the client lives, because some places never or only rarely see snow. So, although the score itself is not critical, the more items that show problem areas, the more driving has been negatively affected. The areas of difficulty that are identified may suggest specific targeted areas for intervention as part of the treatment.

Figure 2.2 shows the TAQ for Paula. Paula is still driving, but she has a great deal of distress when she does. She finds it hard to drive in certain traffic conditions (at night, in heavy traffic) and in certain weather conditions (snow, rain), and she no longer enjoys taking pleasure trips or riding in a car. Clearly, the MVA has affected her current driving. She now experiences a level of anxiety and discomfort that was not present prior to her accident. Paula is experiencing many of the symptoms that have been shown to improve with the type of treatment outlined later.

Figure 2.2 Travel Anxiety Questionnaire (TAQ)

Name: _Paula_ _____   Date: _____

1. Are you driving at the **present** time? (Circle one)

    1. (Yes) Go to question 3
    2. No   Continue to question 2

2. If you are *not* driving presently, why not?
(Check *all* that apply)

    ☐ Driving makes me anxious
    ☐ Physically unable
    ☐ No car
    ☐ No license
    ☐ None of the above

3. Following are eight driving situations. Use the two scales below to **rate how anxious** you are about each situation currently, as well as **how much you avoid** each of these situations **currently.** If the situation does not apply to you please circle "NA" next to the situation.

Anxiety rating scale   0 ——— 1 ——— 2 ——— 3 ——— 4

No anxiety	Very little anxiety	Some anxiety	Moderate anxiety	Severe anxiety

Avoidance rating scale   0 ——— 1 ——— 2 ——— 3 ——— 4

None of the time	Less than half of the time	About half of the time	More than half of the time	All of the time

	Anxiety rating	Avoidance rating	
Driving at night	3	3	NA
Driving in snow			(NA)
Driving in rain	4	2	NA
Highway driving	2	1	NA
Driving in heavy traffic	4	4	NA
Driving in the location of the MVA	4	2	NA
Driving on pleasure trips	2	4	NA
Being the passenger	4	4	NA

Please circle either yes or no:

4. **Currently,** do you restrict your driving speed?   (Yes)   No

5. **Currently,** do you drive only to work?   Yes   (No)

To help in the assessment of depression, we have provided in the client workbook the CES-D (Radloff, 1977). This scale allows us to quantify the severity of depressive symptoms by allowing the client to total the number of items that reflect how he or she is feeling. The CES-D is a 20-item, self-report measure of depression. It was derived from a number of longer psychological instruments to assess depression in the general population, with an emphasis on depressed mood. Individuals are asked to rate how each of the 20 items has applied to them over the past 2 weeks, using a 0- to 3-point scale, where 0 = "rarely or none of the time," 1 = "some or a little of the time," 2 = "occasionally or a moderate amount of the time," and 3 = "most or all of the time."

The CES-D is scored by summing, or adding up, all of the items. In most populations, a score of 16 or higher is consistent with depression. The higher the score the client obtains, the more likely it is that he or she would meet the criteria for the diagnosis of depression. Obviously, some items, such as the presence of suicidal ideation, warrant immediate medical attention.

An explanation of how to understand the CES-D is provided in the example of Cheryl (figure 2.3). Cheryl took the test by answering the questions as to how she felt over the past 2 weeks. She then added up the items. Her total score was 21. This is above the range for suggesting that she is experiencing major depression. It would be our recommendation that she contact her physician or a mental health professional. This decision is particularly important when one considers that the risk of death through suicide needs careful assessment and that help is available. The last two items added to this version of the CES-D are intended to assess the occurrence of thoughts about death and thoughts about harming oneself. They are not added to the total score, but clearly are important. If Cheryl's responses had indicated that she had frequent or strong thoughts about death or harming herself, it would be our recommendation that she immediately seek help from a local medical or mental health professional. Our experience in a clinic setting has been that depression, particularly mild depression, can improve with the treatment offered in this book.

Figure 2.3 Current Center for Epidemiologic Studies–Depression (CES-D)

Name: _Cheryl_   Date: _____

For each statement, please circle the number that best describes how often you have felt or behaved this way during the **past two weeks.**

	Rarely or None of the Time	Some or a Little of the Time	Occasionally or a Moderate Amount of the Time	Most or All of the Time
I was bothered by things that usually don't bother me	0	(1)	2	3
I did not feel like eating; my appetite was poor	0	(1)	2	3
I felt like I could not shake off the blues, even with help from my family or friends	0	1	(2)	3
I felt like I was just as good as other people	(0)	1	2	3
I had trouble keeping my mind on what I was doing	0	(1)	2	3
I felt depressed	0	1	(2)	3
I felt that everything I did was an effort	0	(1)	2	3
I felt hopeful about the future	(0)	1	2	3
I thought my life had been a failure	(0)	1	2	3
I felt fearful	0	(1)	2	3
My sleep was restless	0	1	2	(3)
I was happy	0	1	(2)	3
I talked less than usual	0	(1)	2	3
I felt lonely	(0)	1	2	3
People were unfriendly	(0)	1	2	3
I enjoyed life	0	(1)	2	3
I had crying spells	0	1	(2)	3
I felt sad	0	1	(2)	3
I felt like people disliked me	(0)	1	2	3
I could not get "going"*	0	(1)	2	3
I had thoughts about my death	0	(1)	2	3
I thought about harming myself	(0)	1	2	3
Sum of scores	0	8	10	3
Total score = 21				

*Stop scoring after this item.

Chapter 3 | *Session 1*

(Corresponds to chapters 1, 2, 3, and 4 of the workbook)

Materials Needed

- Completed assessment instruments from the client

- Audiotape to record or share the relaxation exercise

- 11-muscle-group relaxation script

- Form for the MVA description (found in chapter 4 of the workbook)

Session Outline

- Review the client's symptoms and diagnoses.

- Review the client's self-assessment.

- Discuss the normal reaction to trauma, and provide information on PTSD.

- Introduce relaxation training.

- Ask the client to provide a written description of the MVA.

- Discuss the treatment parameters and focus of intervention.

- Assign homework.

Review of Symptoms and Diagnoses

Before this first session, the client should read chapters 1 and 2 of the workbook and complete the self-assessment instruments found in chapter 3 of the workbook.

Although the client has read the introductory chapters on trauma and PTSD, it is important to review the material with him or her during the first session.

The initial session involves a review of the evaluation results with the client. You should use the items from the PCL to guide this portion of the review. Reviewing your client's evaluation serves to foster a sense of understanding of the problem and helps to establish rapport.

Normal Reactions to Trauma and Information on Posttraumatic Stress Disorder

The second goal of this session is to discuss a "normal reaction to trauma." This can be accomplished with the following dialogue:

> *Therapist: It's normal to have some increased anxiety or apprehension when you are in a situation that led to trauma in the past. It's also normal to have some fear or anxiety when you are confronted with situations in which there is potential for harm, or even the threat of death. Thus, although your initial reaction was normal in relation to the severity of your accident, we believe that the symptoms you are experiencing are of sufficient severity and are continuing for a sufficient time that they are causing problems in your daily life. The symptoms that you are having are consistent with a disorder called posttraumatic stress disorder.*

A brief discussion of PTSD is also warranted. Important points to emphasize include the following:

- When the symptoms of anxiety become too great and interfere with your everyday life, they may meet the criteria for a condition called PTSD.

- PTSD includes reexperiencing the trauma, avoidance and numbing to the trauma, and hyperarousal experienced since the time of the trauma.

- While many people associate PTSD with war veterans, the leading cause of PTSD in western civilization is a car crash.

It is also important to provide the client with a psychological understanding of PTSD. We use the two-factor theory of PTSD described by Mowrer (1947) and Keane, Zimering, & Caddell (1985).

The first factor is that trauma can cause a significant amount of distress all by itself. It can be a horrible experience that leaves its own psychological mark. The second factor is that each reminder of the trauma produces a resurgence of anxiety. The feeling of anxiety is so uncomfortable that most people choose to avoid it. Unfortunately, that very common reaction only gives the trauma more strength and increases its power. Because of this understanding of PTSD, almost every empirically derived treatment uses exposure, or helping people to stay with the reminders and memories of the trauma long enough for them to help relearn more normal, less disruptive behavior at those times.

Relaxation Training

The last goal of the first session is to introduce the 11-muscle-group relaxation exercise. Emphasize to your client that relaxation is a skill that will take some time to learn. Explain that it is important to practice this exercise regularly, preferably twice each day.

Ask the client to remove his or her glasses or contact lenses, if applicable, and to loosen any tight clothing. Demonstrate the tension-release cycle with the client's right arm. Inform the client that he or she needs to pay attention to the sensations while tensing and relaxing the various muscle groups, again focusing on the contrast between the two sensations. If the client has a physical injury, caution the client not to tense the muscles in the injured area too hard because that could possibly cause more pain.

The sequence of muscle tension used for the 11-muscle-group relaxation exercise is:

- Right hand and lower arm

- Right upper arm

- Left hand and lower arm

- Left upper arm

- Forehead and eyes

- Lower face and jaw

- Neck and shoulders

- Chest and upper back

- Abdomen and lower back

- Hips, buttocks, and upper legs (right and left)

- Lower legs and feet

11-Muscle-Group Relaxation Script

To begin, find a comfortable position. Please be sure to find a comfortable, quiet place, where you won't be interrupted. To start, gently close your eyes and take a breath. Take a gentle breath in. Hold it, just for a moment, and then relax. Feel the difference. You body tenses slightly as you hold a breath, and then it lets go as you exhale. Find a rhythm that's right for you. Just let the air flow in and out. You may find, as you relax, that your breathing slows down. If it does, just let it happen, and feel the change, as we begin now to focus on the muscles.

Start by making a fist with your right hand. Feel the tension in your hand, across your fingers, your thumb, and your wrist, and into your lower arm. Focus on how the tension feels. Notice the tautness in your fingers, thumb, and wrist. Feel the tension in every fiber, notice all the tension . . . and then relax. Feel the difference. Your fingers may tingle and feel warm. Focus on the change. Some people find that their muscles feel warm and heavy as the relaxation enters. Some find that their muscles grow light as the tension leaves. Notice how it feels for you, and store those feelings away. Contrast how the muscles felt when they were tight . . . and how they feel now, as they let go. Imagine that a wave of relaxation has washed up your arm, touching every muscle and deepening the relaxation. Then imagine that the wave is ebbing away, taking with it all of the tension. Feel the difference, and store those feelings away. Now we move our attention up to the muscles of the upper arm.

Raise your right hand up to touch your shoulder, and then tense the muscles of your upper arm, the biceps and triceps. Feel the tension in these long muscles of the upper arm. Imagine that a band or belt has been pulled tightly around your upper arm, creating tension. Focus on that tension, noticing how every fiber, every muscle feels . . . and then relax. Feel the difference. Notice the contrast between how the muscles felt when they were tight and how they feel now, as they relax. Imagine that the feeling of relaxation has spread up your hand and lower arm, and now is entering your upper arm. Your arm feels heavy . . . warm. Focus on the change. Feel the wave of relaxation washing up your arm, and then ebbing away, bringing deep, complete relaxation. Store those feelings away. Calm. . . . Quiet. . . . Focus on the difference between how the muscles felt when they were tight and how they feel when they are relaxed. Warm . . . heavy. Allowing these feelings to grow without any thought, we'll move our attention across to the left side, starting with the left hand and lower arm.

Make a fist now with your left hand. Feel the tension in your hand, across your fingers, your thumb, and your wrist, and into your lower arm. Focus on how the tension feels. Notice the tautness again in your fingers, thumb, and wrist. Feel the tension in every fiber, and then relax. Feel the difference. The fingers may tingle and feel warm. Focus on the change. Notice how it feels for you, and store those feelings away. Contrast how the muscles felt when they were tight and how they feel now, as they let go. . . . Imagine that a wave of relaxation has again washed up your arm, touching every muscle, but now it's on the left side, deepening the relaxation. Then imagine that the wave is ebbing away, taking with it all of the tension. Feel the difference, and store those feelings away. Now we move our attention up to the muscles of the upper arm.

Raise your left hand up to touch your shoulder, and then tense the muscles of your upper arm, the biceps and triceps. Feel the tension on this side, in these long muscles of the upper arm. Imagine that a band or belt has been pulled tightly around the left upper arm, creating tension. Focus on that tension, noticing how every fiber, every tendon, every muscle feels. Then relax . . . deeply. Feel the difference. Notice the contrast between how the muscles felt when they were tight and how they feel now, as they relax.

Imagine that the feeling of relaxation has spread up your hand and lower arm, and now is entering your upper arm. Heavy . . . warm. Focus on the change. Feel the wave of relaxation washing up your arm, and then ebbing away . . . bringing deep, complete relaxation. Store those feelings away. Calm . . . quiet. Focus on the difference between how the muscles felt when they were tight and how they feel now, when they are relaxed. Warm . . . heavy. Now we move our attention up to the muscles of your face and shoulders.

Let's start with the muscles of your forehead and eyes. Begin to press down with the muscles of your forehead, really tightening your brow and squinting your eyes. Feel all of the tension around your eyes. You have a lot of muscles in this area that allow you to make facial expressions. Feel every muscle. Feel the tension in your forehead, pulling on your temples and around your eyes, even pulling on your scalp . . . and then relax. Let all of the tension go, and focus on the difference. The forehead actually grows longer as it becomes less constricted, more relaxed. It may tingle and feel warm. Notice whatever changes are occurring, and store them away. Feel your eyes relax as the tension lets go and the relaxation deepens and grows. More and more relaxed. Contrast how the muscles felt when they were tight and how they feel now . . . relaxed and calm. Remember those feelings as we move our attention down to your cheeks and jaw.

What I'd like you to do is to bite down with your back teeth and pull the corners of your mouth out, making a tight grimace, a really tight face. If possible, I'd also like you to take your tongue and press it into the roof of your mouth or your front teeth. Hold that tension, feel where the tightness is . . . hold it . . . then relax. Just let go. Let all of the tension leave, and focus on the difference. If the jaw is relaxed all the way, it actually hangs open a little bit, because there's not even enough tension to hold the jaw together. Just let go, completely relaxed. Remember those feelings . . . how your jaw felt when it was tight and how it feels now, when it is relaxed. All of the muscles of your face are relaxing now . . . your forehead . . . your eyes . . . your cheeks . . . and your jaw. Completely relaxed. Now we move our attention down to the muscles of the neck and shoulders.

Again, remember, if you've injured any part of your body, don't aggravate the injury by tensing the muscles so much that they hurt. It's not necessary.

Just be aware of how tension feels and especially how the muscles feel when the tension goes away. That's the memory we want to help you build.

To start, gently press your head back, tensing the muscles in the back of your neck. At the same time, raise your shoulders, making the muscles feel as if there's a knot, as they work against each other. Hold that tightness, and be aware of how the muscles feel tight and hard. Notice where the tension is, feel the tightness . . . then relax. Just let go. Let your head find a comfortable position, resting gently, with no tension holding it up. Let your shoulders relax. Just let the muscles go, loose and calm. Sagging . . . warm and comfortable. Now you should be feeling totally relaxed, letting the warm, comfortable feeling just flow into the area, without any effort at all. Now we move our attention down to the muscles of your chest and upper back.

Here, we're going to create tension a little bit differently. When we start, I'd like you to take a breath and hold it, and then relax when you exhale. When you're ready, take a deep breath, hold it, and then tense the muscles of your chest and upper back. Hold your breath, and feel the tightness of your muscles. A lot of tension is held in this region. Be aware of how the tightness feels and where it is, and then relax. Just exhale, and let all of the tension out. Let your next breath in . . . a slow, comfortable cleansing breath. Let the fresh, clean air in, and as you exhale, let all of the tension leave. You're growing calmer and more deeply relaxed with every breath. Calm . . . peaceful.

Now we move our attention down to the muscles of the stomach and lower back. Here, as with the chest, tense your muscles as you take a breath, hold the breath, and then relax as you exhale. When you're ready, take a deep breath, and as you fill your lungs, press your stomach out, distending it away from your back, feeling the tightness in your abdomen, the sides of your stomach, and even your lower back. Hold the breath, feeling the tautness in your muscles, in the whole trunk region . . . then relax. Just let your breath out, and as you do, let your chest and stomach collapse. As you take your next breath, feel the fresh air fill your lungs, and allow your stomach to rise and fall with your chest. Easily, effortlessly, rising and falling. Each time you exhale, feel your body sink deeply into the cushions. Just let go. Let all of your muscles go limp and loose. Let the cushions hold you, without any effort. As you feel your chest and stomach rise gently, much like an infant who breathes without any tension, feel the relaxation spread into your whole upper body. Calm, peaceful, and deeply relaxed. Think the word "relax" each time you exhale, and feel your body just letting go, with no effort at all. Next we move our attention down to the muscles of your hips and upper legs.

Here, just as when we started, just tighten and relax your muscles, focusing on the contrast between how the muscles feel when they are tight and how they feel as you relax. Start by tightening your hips, your buttocks, and the muscles of your upper legs, the quads and hamstrings. Feel the tautness as you tighten you hips and upper legs. Feel the tightness . . . the tension . . . and hold it. Then relax. Just let go. Feel the change. Again, it may feel as if a warm, comfortable wave has spread over your muscles. As the tension leaves, let yourself sink into the cushions. Imagine the wave of relaxation spreading over the region, and then, as it ebbs away, taking all of the tension with it. Now we move our attention down to your lower legs and feet.

Start here by curling your toes up, creating tension in your toes, the balls of your feet, your ankles, and your calves, on both the right and the left sides. Hold the tension, feel the tightness, and notice how every fiber feels. Then let go. Just relax completely. Imagine all of the tension flowing down and out of your legs, as the relaxation washes up, warm and full, deepening the feeling of calm in every muscle. Just let go, and focus on the change, the contrast between tension and relaxation. Store those feelings away. Remember how they feel, and store that muscle memory away.

Now we're going to go through each muscle group a second time, but this time, we're not going to tighten the muscles. This time, just try to relax your muscles that extra little bit, whenever the muscle is mentioned. Starting where we left off, with the muscles of the feet and lower legs, you feel relaxed . . . quiet.

Upper legs and hips . . . calm . . . comfortable.

Stomach and lower back . . . relaxed. Your breathing is calm and peaceful.

Chest and upper back . . . quiet . . . warm . . . heavy.

Shoulders and neck . . . loose . . . and calm.

Face, down your forehead, across your eyes, down your cheeks and jaw . . . loose . . . heavy.

*Then your arms, down your upper arms, your lower arms . . . and out
your hands and fingers . . . calm . . . peaceful.*

*Now, in your mind, go through your entire body, focusing on relaxation. If
you feel that any muscle group can relax more, try to focus on that group
and deepen the relaxation. . . . No effort, just quiet and calm. Then, focus
on the next five breaths. Just focus on taking a gentle, calm breath. As you
inhale, with each breath, count from one to five, and then, as you exhale,
think the word "relax." Notice yourself growing calmer and more relaxed
with each breath. Take a moment to enjoy those sensations.*

*In a moment, it will be time to come back from this state of relaxation. To
do that, you'll count back in you mind from three to one. With each number, you'll find yourself growing more alert, but still remaining very calm
and comfortable. Three. You're still very calm and comfortable. Two. You're
feeling a little more alert, moving around just a bit, and growing more
aware. One. lowly opening your eyes and feeling alert, yet still very calm
and peaceful.*

As you practice this exercise, you'll find that your relaxation will deepen
and begin to occur sooner.

At the conclusion of the relaxation training, ask the client to rate the
level of relaxation obtained using an 11-point scale (0 = not relaxed;
10 = extremely relaxed). You may also give the client an audiotape of
the exercise (if you recorded your reading of the relaxation script during
the session), or the client can use the relaxation script found in the
workbook.

Written Description of the Motor Vehicle Accident

Conclude the first session by asking the client to provide, by the next session, a written description of his or her MVA. Advise your client to provide a thorough description, including as much detail as possible. Sen-
tence structure and grammar are irrelevant to this assignment. Assure
those clients who insist that they do not have good writing skills that this
is not an "English assignment," but it is an important tool to aid their
treatment.

This treatment is not meant to help clients relieve their pain or physical injuries. If your client is experiencing pain, explain that the focus of the treatment is primarily on the psychological reactions to the MVA. While you realize and acknowledge the problem that pain is causing the client, this treatment is not designed to address pain. Any issues of physical discomfort should be addressed with a medical professional such as an orthopedist, a neurologist, a primary care physician, or a physical therapist.

Homework

Refer the client to the homework diary in the workbook (chapter 4, page 39) to encourage completion of the following tasks. Assignments listed in the diary, other than the following two tasks, will be addressed later.

✎ Practice the 11-muscle-group relaxation exercise twice daily, and record your level of relaxation on a 10-point scale.

✎ Write a thorough description of your MVA.

Chapter 4 | *Session 2*

(Corresponds to chapter 5 of the workbook)

Materials Needed

- Script for the 11-muscle-group relaxation exercise that was conducted at the last session for a repeat of the exercise

Session Outline

- Collect homework from the last session, and review and discuss any compliance issues.

- Have the patient read the MVA description aloud.

- Discuss avoidance and how it relates to PTSD.

- Discuss involvement of the patient's spouse or partner in the treatment.

- Repeat relaxation training.

- Assign homework.

Reading and Elaboration of the Description of the Patient's Motor Vehicle Accident

Begin the second session by asking the patient to read his or her written description of the MVA aloud. Ask questions or make comments as necessary to elicit a thorough and comprehensive response. Remind the patient that it is important to include as much detail as possible in the written account. It is important to note and to point out to the patient his or her reaction to the description, particularly where he or she exhibits discomfort.

Potential Pitfalls

Occasionally, a patient will claim to have "forgotten" the writing assignment. Our recommended response to this situation is to forcefully, but gently, emphasize that the written description is a very important part of treatment, and that the patient must complete it for the next session. It helps to acknowledge that you know that the assignment is difficult.

Avoidance

At this point, a discussion of avoidance should take place. Again, emphasize that avoidance is normal and that it does not signify weakness, but is a normal effort toward adaptation. Remind the patient how avoidance develops, that it is normal, and that, to overcome it, he or she will be asked to face feared situations, both as a driver and as a passenger. Reassure the patient that this process will take place gradually, in small, manageable steps.

Involvement of the Patient's Spouse or Partner in Treatment

The patient is encouraged to bring his or her spouse or partner to the next session (session 3). This is important because the patient's symptoms and this particular treatment protocol may also affect his or her spouse or partner. Reassure the patient that the spouse or partner will be told only what you and the patient agree on regarding the patient's particular symptoms.

Relaxation Training

The 11-muscle-group relaxation exercise is repeated within the session. Once patients have learned how to do the exercise, it is important to help them to understand that, once in a relaxed state, they can begin to think about situations that ordinarily cause anxiety. The patient will feel less arousal when using relaxation. Emphasize that it is important to practice relaxation regularly. You cannot move to the next phase of treatment if the patient has not yet begun to learn the skill through home practice. The goal is to have the patient relax more quickly and deeply each time by using progressively shorter relaxation techniques in subsequent sessions.

Homework

Review the homework diary again, and assign the following tasks:

✎ Read the description of the MVA *aloud* several times daily (at least three times per day), and update the description with new memories as they occur.

✎ Continue to practice the 11-muscle-group relaxation exercise twice daily, and record your level of relaxation on a 11-point scale.

Chapter 5 | *Session 3*

(Corresponds to chapter 6 of the workbook)

Materials Needed

- Travel Hierarchy form

- Positive Coping Self-Statements form

- New audiotape for the 8-muscle-group relaxation exercise

Session Outline

- Collect the homework from the last session, and review and discuss any compliance issues.

- Review the MVA description by having the client read it aloud in session.

- Introduce positive self-coping statements.

- Introduce the travel hierarchy.

- Meet with the client's spouse or partner, if you and the client have agreed to do this.

- Introduce the 8-muscle-group relaxation exercise.

- Assign homework.

Records Review

Every session begins with a review of the homework that the client has completed up until this point. Troubleshoot any difficulty with compliance.

Reading of the Description of the Client's Motor Vehicle Accident

In this session, instruct your client to read his or her MVA description aloud. Review the client's reactions carefully, and discuss them, especially the negative ones. This material is used to introduce the self-talk treatment rationale that is discussed in this session.

Positive Coping Self-Statements

As described in Meichenbaum's (1985) Stress Inoculation Training, the client is instructed in the use of coping self-statements.

Coping self-statements can be used to prepare for stressful situations (e.g., returning to the scene of the MVA, riding in a car); to talk oneself through stressful situations (e.g., while driving); or to reward oneself for facing a stressful situation or plan a better approach to similar situations in the future.

A sample of positive coping self-statements that apply specifically to MVA survivors can be found in the form on page 39. Clients will find a copy in their workbook (chapter 6, page 48).

Travel Hierarchy

At this point in the session, the Travel Hierarchy form is introduced (see sample form on page 40). Instruct the client in how to create a graduated list of travel tasks for in vivo exposure. The client, along with the therapist, negotiates the first steps in the hierarchy, which will be used as homework. It is important to introduce the Subjective Units of Discomfort Scale (SUDS) and to explain how to record these ratings for situations over the next week.

Ask the client to describe 3 to 5 situations now and to continue to add to the list over the next week, until it includes 10 to 15 situations. You may want to ask the client to begin the assignment during this session so that it is clear that the client is able to find and rate situations that are at the lower end, in the middle, and at the upper end of the scale.

Positive Coping Self-Statements

Instructions

Following are some sample statements that you can say to yourself in place of negative "automatic" thoughts that may occur in stressful situations. You can print out this page and keep it with you as a reminder, or you can put a copy in a prominent place until you become familiar with the technique. If you don't find these coping self-statements helpful, there is space on the sheet to add your own. Feel free to try different statements in different situations until you find some that work.

1. *In preparation for stressful situations that you can predict will occur, try the following:*
   (a) What is the specific thing I have to do?
   (b) What plan can I develop for dealing with this?
   (c) This situation is not impossible. I can handle it.
   (d) Don't worry. Worrying isn't going to help anyway.
   (e) I have a great many resources. I can put them to use in this situation.
   (f) What am I scared of?
   (g) I have a lot of support from people who deal with this problem all the time.
   (h) _____
   (i) _____

2. *During the course of a stressful situation, try the following (confrontation and coping):*
   (a) I can manage this situation, if I just take it one step at a time.
   (b) I've gotten through tougher situations than this before. This will not overwhelm me. It just feels that way at times.
   (c) I can see this situation as a challenge or an opportunity to improve, rather than as an annoyance or a burden.
   (d) These are the specific things I need to do to get through the situation (then list the steps).
   (e) Relax. Calm down. I'm in control of this. Take a slow, deep breath.
   (f) Let's keep focused on the present. What do I have to do?
   (g) These feelings are a signal to use the coping skills I'm learning. I can expect the fear to increase, but it will not stop or overwhelm me. This feeling will pass; it always has.
   (h) _____
   (i) _____

3. *After the situation is over, try the following:*
   (a) I need to pay attention to what worked.
   (b) I need to give myself credit for making a good effort and for any improvement, large or small.
   (c) All things considered, I did a good job.
   (d) I'm learning how to deal with this situation more effectively. The next time, I'll do even better.
   (e) I knew I could handle this. It just takes some time, patience, and effort.
   (f) That wasn't as bad as I expected.
   (g) I am making progress.
   (h) _____
   (i) _____

Sample Completed Travel Hierarchy

SUDS Rating

_10_	1. Imagine driving around the block
_30–35_	2. Watch an MVA on television
_40_	3. Sit in the car in the driveway
_60_	4. Drive around a familiar neighborhood
_70_	5. Drive on city streets with moderate traffic
_90_	6. Drive on a highway
_100_	7. Drive past the MVA scene
	8.
	9.
	10.
	11.
	12.

0 = No discomfort
100 = Great discomfort

Involvement of the Client's Spouse or Partner in Treatment

During this session, you should try to meet with your client's spouse or partner. This meeting allows you to gain a fuller sense of the impact of the MVA on the client's behavior and home life and to understand what resources exist, which can aid in treatment. Some spouses or partners may be taking over a great number of tasks that were usually performed by the client before the accident, such as shopping or driving children to activities. This help may have started because the client was physically injured and couldn't perform those tasks. However, this type of help may perpetuate the problem, because it allows the client to avoid potentially anxiety-provoking situations. Meeting with the client's spouse or partner also helps you to corroborate the client's symptoms.

The first portion of the joint session consists of providing information about PTSD, including what it is, how often it occurs, and how it is treated. Present this information in a general fashion, respecting the limit of confidentiality agreed to by the client in session 2.

The major goals of meeting with the client's spouse or partner are as follows:

■ To learn how the client's spouse or partner views the impact of the MVA on the client and his or her family

■ To enlist the support and understanding of the client's spouse or partner by providing specific information about the client's symptoms, as well as an overview of treatment

■ To help the client's spouse or partner to understand the disorder, how the client is trying to get better and how difficult that can be, and how to support the client in that process

Relaxation Training

After the client's spouse or partner is asked to leave, relaxation training is repeated within the session. Now you will introduce the client to a shortened version of progressive muscle relaxation, the eight-muscle-group relaxation exercise. The client is instructed to rate his relaxation using the 11-point scale that he or she has been using all along.

Muscle Groups Used for the 8-Muscle-Group Relaxation Exercise

■ Both arms

■ Both legs and hips

■ Abdomen

■ Chest

■ Shoulders

- Neck

- Eyes and forehead

- Lower face

8-Muscle-Group Relaxation Exercise Script

To begin this exercise, I'd like you make yourself comfortable. In a moment, I'll ask you to close your eyes and just listen to my voice. Then, just let whatever happens happen, without any effort or strain. Just let go. You can't force relaxation, but you can set the stage for it to occur.

Begin now by closing your eyes and focusing on your breathing. Breathe in and out. Find a rhythm that's right for you. Again, you'll notice that, as you relax, your breathing will slow down. Just let it happen, and store away that feeling, if it does occur.

We'll begin the tensing exercise by focusing first on the muscles of your arms, both arms. Start by tensing your hands, your lower arms, and your upper arms. Again, try to hold the tension for about 10 seconds, noticing where the tension is created and really feeling the tightness in your muscles, every fiber. Hold it, being very aware of your fingers, hands, lower arms, and upper arms . . . and then relax. Just let go, and focus on the difference. Contrast how your muscles felt when they were tight and how they feel now. Imagine that the relaxation is spreading up your arm like a wave . . . warm, heavy, quiet, calm. As the wave ebbs, the tension leaves. Store those feelings away, as we move our attention to the lower body . . . the legs and hips.

Here, we'll begin by having you tighten your muscles once again, this time focusing on the entire lower body. Your hips and buttocks are tight and hard, and your upper legs, the quads, the hamstrings, all the way down into the lower legs and feet, are tight and hard. You're really feeling the tension. Then relax, focusing again on the change. Really notice how your muscles feel now . . . warm, calm, and comfortable. Notice the change . . . the contrast between how the muscles felt when they were tight and hard and how they feel now, as they grow calm and loose, peaceful . . . comfortable. Just let the feelings of relaxation wash over you like a wave, full and calm, spreading relaxation into your whole lower body, and then washing the tension away . . . quiet, peaceful. Store those differences away, and then deepen your relaxation. Just let go, more . . . and more . . . as your relaxation gets deeper and deeper.

Now our attention moves to the stomach, focusing on the abdomen and lower back. We'll begin by having you tense your muscles as you take a nice, deep breath. First, fill your lungs. Take a nice, deep, full breath. Hold it, and then tense your stomach by pressing it out, distending it, and feeling the tension in your back, sides, and stomach. Hold it, hold it . . . then relax. Just let go. Let the next breath in be a full, slow breath, and as you exhale, feel any tension leave.

Again, you may feel the muscles grow warm and loose as your relaxation deepens and grows. Whatever you feel, store those feelings away as you notice the difference between how the muscles felt when they were tight and how they feel now, as they relax. Now we'll move our attention up to the muscles of the chest and upper back.

Here, we'll start again with a breath. When you're ready, fill your lungs and tighten the muscles in your chest. Imagine that a belt or band has been pulled tight across your chest. Just notice those feelings. Imagine where the tension is and how it feels to let go and relax. Then, breathe in, a fresh, clean, cleansing breath, and as you exhale, think "relax" . . . in . . . out . . . relax . . . calm.

Now, we move our attention up to the muscles of your shoulders. I'd like you to hunch your shoulders up, tightening them, as you push your shoulder up. Feel the tension in your shoulders, on the right, on the left, and in the lower neck . . . feeling the tightness . . . and then relax. Just let go. Focus on the difference. Feel your shoulders sag and grow limp and loose. Store those feelings away. Just allow the muscles to grow calm, quiet, comfortable, and peaceful. We move our attention now to the neck itself.

Now I'd like you to push your head back, into the cushion, if you're using one, and feel the tension. Notice where the tension is created and how it feels. Hold it, not too hard, but hard enough to feel the tightness, and then relax. Just let go. Let your head find a comfortable position, and settle into that spot deeply and fully, as you focus on the difference. Remember how your muscles felt when they were tight. Again, notice how they feel as they relax, becoming more and more calm and quiet. Now, we move our attention up to the muscles of the face.

We'll begin with the muscles of your forehead and eyes. To begin, squint your eyes, closing them firmly, pulling down on your forehead and temples, really focusing on the muscles of your upper face. Notice where tension is held and how it feels, storing that feeling in your mind, and then relax Just let go, and feel the difference. Focus on the change as the muscles grow longer and loosen. Notice how that feels, and focus on those feelings . . . calm, quiet, and peaceful. Just store those feelings away, as we move to the lower face and jaw.

Now, I'd like you to tighten your jaw by clenching your teeth, pulling your lips back, and pressing your tongue into the roof of your mouth. Notice where the tension is held, hold onto those feelings, and then relax. Just let go, all the way. Your jaw just hangs, loose . . . quiet. Focus on the feeling. Remember the feeling from the earlier exercise, and bring that memory now to mind, deeper and deeper, more and more complete.

In your mind, go through your entire body, from head to toe. Focus on each muscle group, deepening the feeling as you think about each muscle . . . your hands, your arms . . . deeper, relaxed.

Legs, hips . . . quiet, calm.

Stomach, lower back . . . relaxed.

Chest . . . quiet, calm, comfortable.

Shoulders, neck . . . peaceful.

Forehead and eyes . . . loose, limp.

Lower face and jaw . . . quiet, deeply relaxed.

Now, I'd like you to focus on your breathing, and for the next five breaths, count each time you inhale, and then think the word "relax" as you exhale.

One. Breathe in, and then relax. Find your rhythm, your cycle.

Two. Relax.

Three. Relax more deeply.

Four. Relax.

Five. Relax, fully, and deeply.

In a moment, it will be time to open your eyes. Again, we'll count back-
ward from three to one. Each time you practice this exercise, you'll gain
in skill and your relaxation will grow deeper and last longer and longer,
becoming easier and easier to create. But now, we'll start to come back.
Three. You're still very deeply relaxed. Two. You're a little more alert,
maybe moving around just a bit. One. You're all the way back, alert, yet
calm, and very comfortable.

If you like, ask the clients how this exercise worked for them and have
them rate the level of relaxation achieved using the 11-point scale. Be
sure to encourage the clients to practice the relaxation exercise twice
daily. If needed, they can alternate the 8-muscle-group relaxation exercise with the 11-muscle-group relaxation exercise, particularly if they feel
they get better results with the longer exercise.

Homework

Review the homework diary again, and assign the following tasks:

✎ Read the MVA description aloud several times daily (at least three),
and update it with new memories as they occur.

✎ Begin practicing the 8-muscle-group relaxation exercise twice daily,
and record your level of relaxation on a 11-point scale.

✎ Use coping self-statements when necessary.

✎ Continue to add to your travel hierarchy until it contains 10 to 15
items.

Chapter 6 | *Session 4*

(Corresponds to chapter 7 of the workbook)

Materials Needed

- A-B-C-D model and cognitive reappraisal test exercise
- Audiotape for the 4-muscle-group relaxation exercise

Session Outline

- Collect the homework from the last session.
- Review the client's MVA description.
- Review the exposure hierarchy to be certain it includes a wide range of items.
- Introduce cognitive reappraisal.
- Introduce the 4-muscle-group relaxation exercise.
- Assign homework.

Records Review

Every session begins with a review of the client's homework assignments. Up until this point, the homework has included relaxation training, reading of the MVA description, the use of coping self-statements in travel situations, and working on the travel hierarchy. Each of these must be reviewed, and any problems discussed and clarified.

It is crucial that attention is paid to the client's progress on homework up to this point. It is necessary to clear up any misconceptions that could lead to inadvertent heightened anxiety or subsequent escape. Encouragement of the client's steps to this point is critical, and it is important to make sure that the client is cooperative and in agreement with the treatment so far.

Introduction of Cognitive Reappraisal

Cognitive reappraisal is introduced as the client is building on the coping self-statements learned in the last session. At this point, clients are becoming more and more aware of their thoughts, and how they think about a situation can have a significant effect on what they experience and how they subsequently act. In this way, the interpretation of a situation and automatic thoughts can be explained as patterns of appraisal that are learned and can be unlearned.

The use of cognitive reappraisal is introduced using an educational approach. That is, the client is asked to describe a situation in which they experience negative emotions (e.g., anxiety, anger, fear) or engage in a negative behavior (e.g., yelling at someone, crying). They are then asked what they were thinking at the time. These recollections are what will be focused on using cognitive reappraisal.

After the use of cognitive reappraisal has been explained, you should point out the potential impact of the faulty belief system on the client's subsequent emotional and behavioral responses. This is accomplished by using the client's examples and posing questions that challenge the client's beliefs.

Use the following A-B-C-D model described by Ellis (1962) as well as the cognitive reappraisal techniques described by Beck, Rush, Shaw, & Emery (1979) to confront distortions in the client's thinking. Instruct the client to review the discussion of the A-B-C-D model in chapter 7 of the workbook.

The A-B-C-D model depicts the sequence of events that occur when you are trying to change an overly negative interpretation of a situation. The *activating event* (A) is what actually happened during the stressful situation. The *belief* (B) that you have about the situation is how you interpreted it. The *consequence* (C) includes how you felt and how you acted in the situation. Finally, the active part of cognitive reappraisal is how you *dispute* (D), or reevaluate, your "automatic" negative appraisal, with the goal of replacing those maladaptive beliefs and perceptions with more realistic and accurate ones.

Following is an outline of the cognitive reappraisal model:

A = Activating event (What happened?)

B = Belief (What were you thinking when it happened?)

C = Consequence (How did you feel and what did you do in the situation?)

D = Dispute (How might you challenge your overly negative beliefs?)

We know that it takes some time to learn about our thoughts and how they can affect our feelings and behaviors. It is important, however, that you begin to understand that the way you think about something can have a dramatic effect on how you will feel and what you will be able to do. We often attribute anxiety to an external event (e.g., passing the scene of the accident while riding as a passenger, and hearing the screech of brakes). However, the A-B-C-D model begins the process of showing how it is actually our thoughts (e.g., "I can't stand seeing the place where my accident occurred. You shouldn't drive that way; it's awful not to have control when in a car. See, another accident almost happened! I told you it's not safe on the road.") that lead to anxiety, fear, or tension. Some fallacies, or distortions of thinking, can be summarized as a tendency to catastrophize an event and think about the "what if's" that could spell disaster. It doesn't matter that the disaster didn't occur; the fact that it might occur becomes the focus of your reaction. This tendency to overemphasize danger and minimize safety after a car crash is common, and it illustrates how a thought can lead to an undesirable reaction. The same is true of the statement that the squeal of brakes proves that the roads are unsafe. Other possibilities for this sound include a noisy brake pad and a driver stopping in plenty of time, but overreacting. Another example of distorted thinking is seeing the driver of a car as unsafe because you're not driving, even when the driver has a very safe driving record. The thoughts lead to the reaction. Over the next few weeks, try to see if you can identify any thoughts that might be similar to one of the situations discussed earlier or listed as a common problem area. Then see if you can dispute the thought by asking yourself to provide proof of its accuracy or asking yourself if there might be other, more realistic ways to see the same events. Where is the proof that people should drive the way you think they should? It's true that it might be better if more people drove more slowly and maintained more distance between vehicles, for example, but your opinion is unlikely to change the reality of how people drive.

Case Vignette

Cognitive reappraisal is a difficult concept for many people to grasp. You should spend a great deal of time making sure that your client understands how thoughts affect reactions. You can draw on past examples from the client to make this clear, as shown in the following example:

T: You mentioned that, when you got near the mall, you found that your anxiety really grew worse. You started thinking about how there were too many cars, and it seemed likely that you'd have another accident.

C: That's true. I got nervous, and all I could think about was how likely it was that one of those drivers would make a mistake and crash into me!

T: But they didn't crash into you! Your *thinking* about it caused your feelings. Which driver made you nervous? Was there one in particular that stood out? Or was it all the drivers?

C: All the people. The more people, the more likely someone would mess up. It has to be more dangerous.

T: What do you mean by dangerous? The cars are going pretty slowly. If someone hit you, you'd probably survive. In all likelihood, you wouldn't even get hurt, although you would get involved with insurance agents and body shops.

C: But you don't understand! I don't think I could survive another accident. It would be awful, and I know I couldn't stand it!

T: Do you see how, even though nothing happened, you're telling yourself something that is very upsetting. The facts don't really enter into it. You never had a crash at the mall, but the cars seem dangerous when they're all around you like that. You tell yourself how horrible an accident would be, and then you feel horrible. It's not the cars that make you anxious, but how you see them and how you see the situation as dangerous. In fact, you did pretty well. You got there, and then you got home safely. Let's talk about this in a somewhat different way.

Test Exercise for Cognitive Reappraisal

Instruct your client to complete the Test Exercise for Cognitive Reappraisal, which can be found in chapter 7 of their workbook. Answers to the test are provided here, following the text exercise, as well as at the end of chapter 8 in the client workbook.

Review of the Travel Hierarchy

It's important to review how the client is doing with each component of homework. The exposure homework is critical. A client who has anxiety and PTSD following a car crash often tries to avoid or reduce anxiety by staying away from anxiety-producing situations. In this session, you want to make sure that the client is addressing the graded steps for exposure in the way that makes the most sense. You can bring up this topic by saying something such as, "Let's see how the past week went with the driving exposure hierarchy."

Just as there can be considerable variability in the impact of an MVA on driving, the length of treatment for this particular problem may vary. It is not uncommon for a client to need several weeks of sessions to adequately attend to each aspect of the exposure hierarchy. If the client seems

Test Exercise for Cognitive Reappraisal

We have now set up a series of situations we would like you to try to apply either coping self-statements or the A-B-C-D model to see how well you have learned them. Answers are provided at the end of this chapter.

John was driving to the store when suddenly the car in front of him cut him off. John became angry. He started yelling, "How dare you! You're supposed to signal before you change lanes! You could have killed me!

What possible distortions did John make in his appraisal of the scene? How could he dispute these distortions? Use the A-B-C-D model:

A = Activating event: _____

_____

B = Belief: _____

_____

C = Consequence: _____

_____

D = Dispute: _____

_____

Mary was riding in the car with her husband Pete. Pete has always been a good driver. He's never been in an accident. However, since her accident, Mary now finds Pete is just too aggressive. He drives too fast and gets too close to the cars in front of them. Several times during each ride she'll have to tell Pete to slow down, that he's too close, and that he'd be in a terrible accident if the other driver stopped without warning.

What is Mary telling herself that is raising her level of concern? How can she dispute these ideas?

A = Activating event: _____

_____

B = Belief: _____

_____

C = Consequence: _____

_____

D = Dispute: _____

_____

Sally has had several panic attacks and now is worried that one would come when driving. If she were to have a panic attack while driving, she knew it would lead to an accident and probably kill her.

Identify the A-B-C's and Dispute:

A = Activating event: _____

_____

B = Belief: _____

_____

C = Consequence: _____

_____

D = Dispute:

_____

Cheryl didn't tell her husband, but she started worrying about getting into another accident. The drivers on the road just seemed out of control. It was just a matter of time before one hit her again. The next accident, she knew, would be fatal. How could she leave the house?

Identify the A-B-C's and Dispute:

A = Activating event: _____

_____

B = Belief: _____

_____

C = Consequence: _____

_____

D = Dispute:

_____

Answers to Cognitive Reappraisal Test Exercise

John

A = *Activating Event:* Car cut him off

B = *Belief:* "You don't act like I want you to! You should follow the rules!"

C = *Consequence:* Anger and upset

D = *Dispute:* Who says the world will follow the rules? Does everyone follow the rules? I don't think so. Do you need to get upset at everyone? Were you in that much danger? You saw it coming, you did avoid them.

Mary

A = Husband drives too fast

B = It's dangerous, we can have a terrible accident.

C = Anxiousness

D = I'm magnifying the danger and forgetting what a good driver Pete has been.

Sally

A = Panic attack, worry of panic attacks

B = Next panic attack will lead to an accident and probably kill her.

C = Worry, anxiety, and fear

D = Even if you panic, how do you know the next one will kill you? You could pull over and deal with it. You are learning skills to control panic, use them. The worry heightens the anxiety.

Cheryl

A = Other drivers are too dangerous

B = If I leave the house, its just a matter of time until I get in an accident that will be fatal

C = Worry and fear

D = You're reading the future. You don't know if any of those thoughts are true. You are magnifying the danger and minimizing your own skills and statistics regarding fatalities.

stuck and is making little progress with an item from the hierarchy, imaginal desensitization can also be used before in vivo exposure. It may be helpful at times for the therapist to accompany the client in the vehicle while he or she is attempting particularly distressing driving situations. During driving tasks, it is important to be positive and reassuring, and to model coping self-statements or cognitive reappraisal techniques, as appropriate.

4-Muscle-Group Relaxation Exercise

Now you will introduce the client to a briefer version of progressive muscle relaxation, the four-muscle-group relaxation exercise. Be sure to rate the client's response to the relaxation using the BRRS scale. The client is instructed to rate his or her relaxation using the 11-point scale that he or she has been using all along.

Clients who have difficulty transitioning to this shorter technique should return to the 8-muscle-group relaxation sequence and use the 4-muscle-group exercise after the longer exercise. Clients may also try the 4-muscle-group relaxation exercise, adding or using the 8-muscle-group exercise only if they believe that it will deepen their relaxation.

4-Muscle-Group Relaxation Script

Start by finding a comfortable position. Settle down, close your eyes, and take a breath. Fill your lungs with fresh, clean air, and when you're ready, exhale. Try to find a rhythm to your breathing that is comfortable for you. Rising and falling, very comfortable. Begin to think of the word "relax" every time you exhale, and feel the relaxation beginning to spread throughout your body.

Begin the exercise by starting to focus on your hands and arms on both the right and left sides. I would like you to start by making a fist, first with your right hand and then with your left hand, tensing both arms. Feel the tension across your fingers, thumb, wrist, and forearm. Feel the tension all the way up both arms, on the right and left sides. Hold that tension. Be very aware of that tension . . . holding it, noticing it . . . and notice where all the tightness is held. Then relax. Focus on the difference. Focus on the difference between where you felt the tension and how the relaxation is growing.

Imagine the relaxation feeling as if a wave has just washed up your arm, bringing a warm and comfortable sensation wherever it touches, and as it ebbs away, taking all of the tension with it. Some people find that, when the relaxation grows deep, the arm feels warm and heavy. Other people feel that it grows light as the tension leaves. Whatever it feels like for you, store away those feelings. Now we'll move our attention down to the muscles in the lower body.

The next step is to tense the muscles in your legs, feet, hips, and buttocks all at once. To do this, start by tensing your feet. Curl your toes, and tense your toes, the balls of your feet, and your ankles and calves, right up into your thighs, pressing your legs hard, right into your hips and buttocks, pressing down so that your entire lower body is made hard and firm. Feel the tightness. Be very aware of these sensations. Hold the tightness, notice it, being very aware of where all of the tightness is held, and then relax. Just let it go. As you let it go, let all of the tension leave. Let the relaxation enter. Again, focus on the difference. Feel the relaxation washing over you, like a warm, comfortable wave, bringing deep, full relaxation, and as it ebbs away, taking all of the tension with it. You're feeling calm, quiet, and peaceful. Allow those feelings to deepen and grow. With the next few breaths, every time you exhale, feel the relaxation spreading down, deeper and deeper, as you become more relaxed with every breath.

Now, move your attention up to the muscles in your stomach and chest. You are going to create tension a little differently here. Start with a good, deep breath, and then tighten the muscles, hold your breath, and relax as you exhale. Whenever you're ready, take a good, deep breath, filling your lungs. As you fill your lungs, hold the tightness. Feel the tightness like a band or belt placed around your chest, and hold the tight feeling in your stomach. Tense the muscles in your abdomen, being very aware of all of the tension there. Hold the tightness, being very aware of where the tautness is held, and whenever you are ready, slowly exhale. Imagine the next breath in as a fresh, clean cleansing breath. As you exhale, just imagine all of the tightness leaving. Also, notice that when you fill your lungs, your stomach rises with your chest. As you exhale, feel your stomach sink with your chest.

Focus on the middle of your trunk. You're breathing from your diaphragm, as your chest and stomach rise as one and empty as one. Relax those muscles all the way, sink deeply into the cushion, and let all of the tension leave. Let the relaxation grow deeper and deeper as you feel more and more relaxed. We will come back to this breathing in just a few moments. It's very important that you learn to relax your chest and stomach by controlling your breathing.

Now we will move to the muscles in your shoulders, neck, face, and scalp. Start by pressing your head back, and then raise your shoulders, press your forehead down, squint your eyes, and clench your jaw, so that all of the muscles in this area are hard and firm. Feel the tightness, being aware of the sensations, and then relax. Just let it go. As you let all of the tension leave, let your shoulders sag, as you feel calm and quiet. Your forehead grows smooth as the muscles grow longer and become less constricted. You may feel tingling and warmth in the muscles. Whatever you feel, just focus on those sensations, deepen them, and let them grow, as your relaxation grows deeper and deeper.

We have gone through all of the muscles once, and we will go through them a second time. This time, don't tighten the muscles. Just focus on them, trying to relax them just a little bit. Forehead, eyes, relaxed and calm. Lower face and jaw, loose, comfortable. Your neck and shoulders are growing relaxed and heavy, peaceful, and quiet. Your chest and upper back are relaxed, and your breathing is full and calm. Every time you exhale, just imagine the relaxation spreading throughout your body. Just feel your chest and stomach rising and falling, feeling calmer and calmer with every breath. Your hips and upper legs are relaxed and heavy, and your lower legs and feet are relaxed. All of the tension is draining down and out, as your relaxation deepens and grows. Your arms, down your upper arms, down your lower arms, and out your hands and fingers. Relaxed and calm.

In your mind, go through your body, from head to toe. Wherever you feel tension, try to release it, as your relaxation becomes even deeper and you feel calmer and quieter, more and more relaxed. Focus on your breathing, rising and falling, filling your lungs very naturally and comfortably. As you relax, feel yourself sinking into the cushions, feeling very, very calm and very, very peaceful.

Now imagine yourself in a very relaxing place. As completely and vividly as you can, I would like you to create that place. Imagine yourself there now, in a warm, comfortable, quiet place. Feel the sun, see the color of the sky, see the clouds or birds, see the water, smell the water, and hear whether it's waves or a stream. You're lying on a beach. Feel the warmth and grit of the sand beneath you. You're lying on grass. Feel the coolness of it. Whatever is there, just create it vividly, fully, with your mind, and enjoy the feelings you are experiencing. Find a spot or place that is memorable, one that is easy to recall. Every time you do the relaxation exercise, as you become deeply relaxed, I would like you to think of this place, this image, or this scene. Imagine how deeply relaxed you would be if you were there. Remember those feelings, remember the contrast between how you felt when your muscles were tight and how you feel when you are fully relaxed. Now it's time to come back, as I count backward from three to one. When I get to one, slowly open your eyes, coming all the way back, but continue to remember deep and full relaxation. Three. You're starting to come out. You're still very, very comfortable. Two. You're a little more alert, perhaps moving around just a bit. One. You're all the way back. Slowly open your eyes, feeling alert, calm, and quiet.

Homework

Review the homework diary again, and assign the following tasks:

✎ Read the MVA description aloud several times daily (at least three times), and update it with new memories as they occur.

✎ Begin the exposure exercises, first using imaginal exposure and then using in vivo exposure. Record your negative thoughts and coping self-statements for discussion in the next session.

✎ Practice cognitive reappraisal skills and complete the Test Exercise for Cognitive Reappraisal.

✎ Begin practicing the 4-muscle-group relaxation exercise, and record your level of relaxation on an 11-point scale.

Chapter 7 *Session 5*

(Corresponds to chapter 8 of the workbook)

Session Outline

▪ Collect the homework from the last session.

▪ Review the client's MVA description.

▪ Review the client's Test Exercise for Cognitive Reappraisal.

▪ Review the travel exposure hierarchy, and apply cognitive-behavioral techniques.

▪ Introduce the relaxation-by-recall technique.

▪ Assign homework.

Records Review

Begin the session by reviewing the client's homework assignments, and then ask the client to read the MVA description aloud. By this point, reading the MVA description may begin to feel boring and repetitive to the client, and he or she may no longer report having a substantial reaction. If the client spontaneously states that this is the case, you can tell the client to begin reading the MVA description just once per day; otherwise they should continue reading it three times per day.

Application of Cognitive-Behavioral Skills

Most of this session is spent discussing the travel hierarchy and the client's exposure exercises. The focus of treatment becomes more and more the application of CBT skills. It is important to review all homework thoroughly and to discuss with the client how he or she is dealing with the tasks in the driving hierarchy and the changes in his or her life. Encourage your client to bring his or her homework records to every session.

As clients encounter new and related situations, they should use coping and cognitive strategies to manage their anxiety and plan for the future. They can use imaginal exposure techniques for situations that rarely occur or are difficult to recreate (e.g., getting cut off in traffic, close calls while driving). Usually, most of this session is spent discussing self-talk, addressing cognitive distortions, and problem-solving. Remind the client to make notes in the homework diary for discussion in the next session.

Relaxation-by-Recall

Guide your client through the four-muscle-group relaxation exercise. After you complete this exercise, inform your client that you will take him or her through it one more time, but this time, just by recall. This time, your client will relax his or her muscles by remembering, or recalling, how the muscle groups felt when they were relaxed. Ask the client to signal you by raising the right forefinger if he or she is not able to relax a particular muscle group. Go through the same four muscle groups, asking your client to pay attention to that particular muscle group and identify any feelings or sensations of tension or tightness.

If the client is successful at learning the relaxation-by-recall technique, instruct him or her to try it at home, using the four-muscle-group relaxation exercise as a supplemental technique. Clients who struggle with this new method should be instructed to continue with the relaxation techniques that they have been using up to this point. You will readdress relaxation-by-recall in the next session.

Review the homework diary again, and assign the following tasks:

✎ Continue to read the MVA description several times daily. Clients who are bored with this assignment can be instructed to read it only once per day for the remainder of treatment.

✎ Continue exposure exercises, using both imaginal and in vivo exposure. Negotiate items to be tried on the travel hierarchy.

✎ Begin practicing the relaxation-by-recall technique, and record your level of relaxation on a 11-point scale. Clients who are not successful with this method may continue to use the relaxation techniques that they have learned up until this point.

✎ Complete the midtreatment assessment in chapter 9 of the workbook, including the PCL, CES-D, and TAQ, and bring the completed assessment to the next session.

Chapter 8   *Session 6*

(Corresponds to chapter 10 of the workbook)

Session Outline

- Collect the homework from the last session.

- Collect and review the midtreatment reassessment.

- Reduce the client's reading of the MVA description.

- Review the travel exposure hierarchy, and apply cognitive-behavioral techniques.

- Introduce the cue-controlled relaxation technique.

- Assign homework.

Records Review

As with every session, begin by reviewing the homework assignments and having the client read the MVA description. As mentioned in chapter 7, if the client has become bored with this task, it can be reduced to one time per day or less. It is important not to stop this part of the treatment prematurely, however. Use your judgment.

You will also review the client's completed midtreatment assessment to assess his or her progress up until this point. The questionnaires allow you to measure changes in the areas of anxiety (PTSD), mood (depression), and driving (travel anxiety).

Travel Hierarchy

The travel hierarchy continues to be the focus of treatment. By this point, the client may understand the basic ideas of providing graduated in vivo exposure, correcting negative self-talk, and even spotting and correcting cognitive fallacies. A client who has mastered these ideas may need more of the same, with your support and occasional guidance. It is your role to apply gentle, yet firm pressure to your client to continue up the hierarchy.

Other clients may take longer to work their way up the hierarchy. There may be several reasons, including difficulty correcting negative self-talk or understanding logical fallacies. Also, some people simply progress up the hierarchy more slowly than others. If a client seems a bit stuck, you might need to help them find intermediate steps between two hierarchy points.

In this session, it is important to discuss the driving hierarchy tasks and the thoughts that exposures elicit.

Cue-Controlled Relaxation

In this session, you will repeat the relaxation-by-recall technique that was introduced in the last session. If the client has been successful with that technique, then cue-controlled relaxation is explained. Cue-controlled relaxation is a method to help the client relax quickly and efficiently in all situations that may arise.

Teach this relaxation technique by having the client take a deep breath and pair exhalation with the word "relax." This is done first with the client's eyes open and then with the eyes closed.

You may also encourage your client to use imagery. Ask the client to think of some situations that are tied to images or memories of being deeply relaxed. Have the client perform cue-controlled relaxation as many times as possible per day (a minimum of 12), until it becomes automatic. Suggest that the client practice this relaxation technique while doing everyday activities, such as stopping at a traffic light, drinking from a cup, or hanging up the telephone after a conversation.

Review the homework diary again, and assign the following tasks:

✎ Continue to read the MVA description daily. If the client is bored with this assignment, instruct him or her to read it only once per day for the remainder of treatment.

✎ Continue the exposure exercises, using both imaginal and in vivo exposure. Negotiate items on the travel anxiety hierarchy.

✎ If the client is having trouble with the exposure homework, encourage them to stay with it. One can focus on this differently, as needed, in future sessions.

✎ Begin practicing cue-controlled relaxation at least 12 times per day, and record your level of relaxation on an 11-point scale.

Chapter 9 | *Session 7*

(Corresponds to chapter 11 of the workbook)

Materials Needed

- Pleasant events list (found in workbook chapter 11)
- Anger sheet (found in workbook chapter 11)

Session Outline

- Collect the homework from the last session.
- Discontinue reading of the MVA description if the client reports no emotional physiological reaction to reading it.
- Continue exposure homework on the items that are ranked higher in the travel hierarchy.
- Broaden the focus of treatment to potentially address the following issues (not all people will have all of these issues):

  Psychic numbing

  Existential issues

  Estrangement, social isolation, and depression

  Anger
- Introduce pleasant events scheduling.
- Assign homework.

Records Review

During every session, all of the relevant homework assignments are reviewed. Some tasks may diminish greatly in importance, however, including reading the MVA description aloud and possibly some of the travel exposure.

Treating Clients Who Have Psychic Numbing

If your client is experiencing psychic numbing, begin this session by explaining that numbing is an avoidance behavior. Feelings related to the numbing are discussed in this session, as well as any possible signs of depression.

Your client may describe feeling overwhelmed by the enormity of the MVA and the effect it had on his or her life. The client may feel cut off from others or their former selves and somehow different. He or she may not be as interested in forming and maintaining relationships as in the past. These feelings are all part of psychic numbing.

Encourage your client to take small steps to reengage in pleasurable activities. Pleasant event scheduling is important for this type of intervention.

Treating Clients Who Have Estrangement and Social Isolation

Estrangement occurs when people experience few positive events and tend to isolate themselves from social situations. If your client has been avoiding family and friends and pleasurable activities, a formal program of reaching out to social contacts is described and planned in this part of the session. Keep in mind that clients often have an excuse or explanation for why they have given up social activities. Explain to the client that it is important to do things now that may bring pleasure because engaging in those activities will make him or her feel better. The client will not just feel better spontaneously.

Homework assignments, such as calling or visiting designated people, even without a strong desire to do so, are an important part of the treatment of estrangement and social isolation. Pleasant events scheduling is an ideal intervention for the client experiencing isolation as well.

Pleasant Events Scheduling

Often, when a therapist asks a client to identify an activity that he or she used to enjoy before the MVA, the client will say something such as, "When I feel better, I will try to get back to _____ (pleasurable activity)." The therapist should then respond, "No, you have it backward. After you return to _____ (pleasant event), you will begin to feel better."

When assigning activities that the client once enjoyed as homework, it is preferable to select activities that are done with other people instead of solitary activities, if possible.

A list is provided in the workbook (chapter 11) of activities that are generally considered positive. Most people can identify a number of events or activities that often leave them feeling happier or more positive. Ask your client to read the list in chapter 11 of the workbook and identify a few events that he or she might want to try. There is space provided at the end of the list for your client to add some activities that he or she may have enjoyed in the past or might enjoy now. Once the client reaches this point in the program, instruct him or her to try to schedule at least one pleasant event each day.

Pleasant Events Practice Sheet

The pleasant events practice sheet (found in chapter 11 of the workbook) is designed to help your client incorporate pleasant events into his or her daily life. Instruct your client to complete this form as homework.

Treating Clients Who Have Existential Issues

One of the dominant themes found among some MVA survivors is the fear of death, accompanied by intrusive reminders of one's mortality. While it would be possible to treat this fear as simply a cognition, using the methods outlined in earlier chapters, we found it more useful to explore these issues in what one could term a "personally meaningful way."

Early psychologists believed that the fear of one's own mortality is universal. Near-death experiences can be unsettling and may cause heightened anxiety in daily life. Some clients have beliefs about an afterlife. While some are comforted by their faith, others face doubt or believe that there is no life after this one. Therefore, they focus on the fragility of their life and are distressed by how quickly everything can change. Others focus on unfinished goals. Many of us have plans for our lives and assume that we have the time to accomplish them; however, an accident can make it all too clear that this can be changed without any consideration of our own wants and ideas.

After speaking with many survivors, we have come to the conclusion that the time spent in soul-searching and examining these questions is important. An accident can give your client a chance to reorganize and refocus his or her life. Priorities can be examined, and changes in daily life can be made.

"What if I had died?" For many MVA survivors, this is more than a rhetorical question. They know that they really could have died. It's a meaningful question, with an emotional component. However, rather than being dismayed by the losses that their death might have caused, survivors have the opportunity to affirm their place and act on the insights that this line of thinking brings.

"What if someone else died?" Some MVAs cause fatalities, either in the client's car or in another vehicle. The sense of responsibility and the feelings associated with this tragic situation cannot be underestimated. Besides the personal sense of responsibility that is often associated with the MVA, society imparts its own sanctions on individuals, with legal action and possible imprisonment or other punishment. The stress associated with these situations compounds an already difficult, if not seemingly impossible, situation. As psychologists, we cannot determine or judge what is just. Individuals and society must try to determine what is right and understandable for them. Some individuals take from an MVA a sense of responsibility to help others. Others have carried the weight of the tragedy throughout their lives in a very negative and self-defeating fashion. When these individuals are seen in a professional setting, no judgment is rendered regarding these actions. No one planned or intended for tragedies to occur. Accidents are just that, accidents. Whatever responsibilities are assumed as part of the accident, each individual will carry them alone. Some individuals we have worked with have demonstrated punitive self-appraisals when, in fact, the circumstances did not suggest that they were as responsible as they believed they were. However, it is normal for each of us to ask, "What if I had done this?" or to say, "If only I had done this instead of that," as part of our self-evaluation. A driver may ask himself whether he might have prevented the tragedy. Drivers ask questions such as, "If I'd had a better grasp on the steering wheel, would I have been able to swerve out of the way?" or "If only I had pressed on the brakes a little harder, would they have stopped in time?" or "If only I had left a minute later, would the accident have been prevented altogether?" Each of these self-statements can lead to self-recrimination and guilt that can make it hard for the survivor to recover emotionally from the accident.

It has been our experience that individuals who have been involved in fatal MVAs were more likely to have psychological problems in the aftermath and have benefited from professional intervention. Psychologists, social workers, and psychiatrists are well trained to deal with grief, depression, and the psychological effects of trauma. We have found it helpful to explore questions with clients regarding their mortality and underlying beliefs and fears.

If you feel uncomfortable discussing issues of spirituality and religion, you should refer your client to a priest or clergy member within the community.

Treating Clients Who Have Anger Management Difficulties

One of the major symptoms of PTSD is increased irritability, anger, and hostility. Additionally, the circumstances surrounding an MVA can lead to situations in which most individuals would become angry and upset. Clients may experience a sense of injustice when what happens it at odds with their internal beliefs, or it may be that the legal system itself is set up to cause revictimization. Revictimization can occur when clients are sent to insurance company doctors or asked to complete depositions that can be adversarial, confrontational, and very distressing. Individuals who feel that they have been wronged from the start by being a victim in an MVA may feel helpless, hopeless, and frustrated in dealing with a system that is not always responsive to their financial, emotional, and physical needs.

We see difficulty with anger management as difficulty in managing a strong affect. Rather than suppressing or controlling the emotion, as happens with emotional numbing or suppression of feeling after a trauma, some survivors have difficulty modulating the expression of their anger, which may then be uncontrolled and excessive.

Anger may be directed at the other driver. Many victims feel that they were not responsible for the accident and, in fact, were not found to be legally responsible when the facts were examined. For example a driver may have been stopped at a traffic light, minding her own business, when another car crashed into her from behind, at a high rate of speed. She was hurt, her vehicle was wrecked, and now she is suffering through no fault of her own. In cases such as this, clients may find themselves angry at the system.

Insurance companies, as part of their need for documentation, may withhold payment until all necessary examinations are completed. The examinations may not always lead to a decision that is favorable to the victim, or the decision may not be made in a timely manner. Lawyers, litigation, and the process that is used within the United States for dealing with personal injury can be very adversarial. If they are expecting to receive either compensation or benefits, victims are required to comply with all examinations and requests, even for seemingly personal and irrelevant information. Survivors sometimes feel as if they are "on trial," when they see themselves as the victim and the injured party. At times, they may leave examinations with physicians or other medical professionals feeling as if they were mistreated or in some way held in contempt. They may get the impression that the medical professional believes that their injuries have lasted longer than they should or have presented in ways that the doctors find hard to explain. They may feel as if each question is a test of their veracity and that they need to convince the examiner of the validity of their injuries.

Cognitive techniques are often used to try to deal with the underlying assumptions of justice and fairness that are contributing to the client's anger. These techniques are used as another way to try to control the subsequent response and deal with the emotional reactivity.

One of the most straightforward interventions for anger uses a cognitive model similar to the one outlined earlier in this book. The client may have no verbally mediating self-statements to stop the occurrence of anger; may have very negative, revengeful automatic thoughts and irrational beliefs; or may have limited social skills for dealing with these problems other than through the expression of anger. Each of these reasons would require a different approach to the management of anger. Each would require addressing the client's idiosyncratic thoughts or beliefs about the situation and changing these thoughts with techniques, such as the ones learned in sessions 3 and 4. Your client may use the Anger Situations Worksheet in the workbook (chapter 11) to practice changing his or her initial reactions to anger-provoking situations.

Encouraging clients to use cognitive coping statements (e.g., "Don't assume the worst." "Try to predict situations before they occur and decide how you might act.") has been helpful in helping clients to deal with anger-provoking situations. Reviewing the A-B-C-D model of Albert Ellis may help to clarify underlying thoughts, such as being treated unfairly and feeling as if "this is just awful and is never going to get better." Thoughts related to how the client believes that he has been treated, his stamina and endurance, and the fairness of life can all be challenged and restructured.

Relaxation skills can also be used to help the client deal with anger. Instruct your client to use the brief relaxation techniques employed throughout the treatment. This will give him or her some time to apply the cognitive techniques discussed earlier. Many people who become angry seem to hold some of the following views about the world. They may overestimate the probability of a negative event and underestimate their personal or other coping resources. They may also have polarized ideas, such as that things are either good or bad, right or wrong, and they may overgeneralize, reaching broad, sweeping conclusions, such as "Everybody is dumb," "All drivers are awful," and "All of them are worthless." They may also have some type of inflammatory thinking, such as labeling events or people in a highly negative way. Catastrophizing, or casting

Anger Situations Worksheet

You can use the following situations to practice how you might deal with frustration and anger by changing either your initial reactions or your subsequent reactions.

Situation 1. While you are driving, another driver comes up behind you, tailgates for several minutes, pulls around you and angrily gives you the finger, and then pulls in front of you and slows down.

Describe your thoughts, possible ways to deal with the situation, and your ideas for how to prevent it from happening again.

_____

_____

_____

_____

_____

Situation 2. You are asked to undergo an independent medical examination. You just had a number of examinations by your own doctor, and you wonder why they just can't take your doctor's test results and opinions as they are intended. You don't want to have this examination, and you are afraid that it will mean cutting off your disability funds and a decision that will negatively affect your life.

Describe your reaction.

_____

_____

_____

_____

How could you challenge your thoughts about this situation?

_____

_____

_____

_____

_____

_____

Situation 3. You don't feel well. Your neck has been bothering you all day. Medication has not helped the pain, and you slept poorly the night before. Your child comes in from school very excitedly and jumps on your lap. This produces more pain. You have told your child many times to be careful around you because of your injuries, but he or she does not seem to listen.

What is your initial reaction?

_____

_____

_____

_____

_____

What are your thoughts?

_____

_____

_____

_____

_____

What are some possible alternative thoughts?

_____

_____

_____

_____

_____

What are some possible alternative reactions?

_____

_____

_____

_____

_____

Situation 1

Your immediate thought: "This jerk is dangerous. He has no business doing this: I need to take care of him before he hurts me. What an idiot!"

You can prevent these thoughts: "Okay, this guy is a bad driver. Is it worth getting in a fight over it? Even if I stop him, there are more bad drivers out there."

Contol yourself and take a deep breath: "He'll be gone in a minute, and I can get back to my driving."

Situation 2

Your immediate reaction might be to feel anger, fear, and anxiety.

You can challenge your thoughts: "This is just an independent medical examination. I don't know how it's going to turn out. I have a lot of good doctors who are in my corner, trying to get me better. Whatever this person does, good or bad, I can deal with it. I don't have to catastrophize the outcome before anything really even happens."

Situation 3

Your initial reaction might be anger, and you might think, "I don't need this. This is too much. I can't take any more of this!"

Possible alternative thoughts and reactions could be one or both of the following:

"It's been a bad day. I've dealt with this before. The pain does change. Let's try to relax and use whatever I can to help me cope."

"Kids don't always listen That's why they're kids. It would have been better if he hadn't jumped on me and hurt me, but I'm glad he loves me. Maybe I need to figure out another way to get him to listen more often. We've got time. It hurt, but I'll survive."

events in an extremely negative light, can also result in angry responses. Demanding and commanding ways, such as believing that their preferences and desires have more worth or merit than those of others, can lead to anger. Additionally, ideas about how things ought to have been, have to be, or should be, can lead to anger. It is important for you to work with your client to achieve a more balanced perspective.

Homework

From this point on, treatment can become more flexible. Some clients need to focus on issues of anger, others still require significant focus on driving behaviors, and so on.

✎ Assign the Anger Situations Worksheet if it is appropriate to your client's needs.

Chapter 10 *Sessions 8 and 9*

(Corresponds to chapter 11 of the workbook)

Session Outline

- Collect the homework from the last session.

- Review cognitive restructuring, as appropriate.

- Continue with exposure and imaginal treatment, as warranted.

- Continue with treatment of individual themes, as identified.

Records Review

Check on the client's progress with driving and the travel avoidance hierarchy. Review the client's pleasant events schedule, and find out if the client has resumed social contact and involvement, at least as noted in the homework. Discuss the client's reactions. If the client has not yet resumed social activity, strongly encourage him or her to do so.

Individual Themes

In these sessions, you will continue the discussion that was started in the previous session (session 7) of the themes that are relevant to your particular client. Your client may be experiencing one or more of the following:

- Psychic numbing

- Estrangement, social isolation, and depression

- Existential issues

- Anger

If your client is experiencing difficulty in any of these areas, begin to explore possible cognitive schema related to depression, such as faulty logic, and apply cognitive restructuring. Explore possible avoidance of strong affect, and if possible, develop methods outside or within the treatment the session to increase therapeutic exposure to those effects.

Homework

- At this point, you may tell your client to discontinue reading the MVA description aloud, if you believe that he or she has achieved the maximum benefit from this exercise.

- Continue the exposure to items on the travel hierarchy, including the SUDS rating, so that the therapist can monitor the decrease in distress associated with repetition. By this time, most clients are able to visit the site of their MVA. Such a visit, if at all feasible, is much encouraged.

- Continue the relaxation practice.

- Continue to engage in pleasant events and social activities.

- Complete the reassessment in workbook chapter 12 for session 10.

- The focus is now on the client's specifically targeted areas of intervention.

Chapter 11 | *Session 10*

(Corresponds to chapters 12 and 13 of the workbook)

Materials Needed

- Completed posttreatment assessment instruments from the client

Session Outline

- Review the client's posttreatment assessment (PCL, CES-D, and TAQ) to help determine the need for and focus of additional treatment.

- Review all treatment procedures.

- Review avoidance behavior.

- Review the relaxation techniques that the client has learned.

- Review coping self-statements.

- Review cognitive reappraisal techniques.

- Review pleasant events scheduling and social interaction.

- Review other important themes in treatment (discussed in the previous three sessions).

Final Session

In the last few sessions, you have worked with your client to individualize his or her treatment. Flexibility is important during the final sessions, and the length of treatment should be adjusted according to the client's progress and individual needs. As you can see from the earlier list, review of the posttreatment assessment will help the therapist to determine how much more treatment, if any, is needed. If the questionnaires suggest that the client still has issues of depression or travel anxiety or symptom clusters associated with PTSD, a plan should be outlined and discussed with the client. The format of treatment can easily be modified, and the length of treatment may vary from one client to the next. Although less common, it is possible for a client to undergo treatment for more than a year.

At the termination of treatment, the therapist should discuss the possibility of further needs in the future, and he or she should encourage the client to return for treatment, if necessary.

As with any therapy, spend some time discussing termination with the client. You may want to tell the client how pleased you are with his or her progress and with all of the hard work that he or she did to complete the treatment program. Let your client know that he or she can maintain the gains experienced in treatment by continuing to use the newly learned skills to counteract any tendency to fall back into the behavior of avoiding travel or social interactions. Urge your client to continue to attempt difficult driving situations. Also urge him or her to continue to be aware of negative thoughts and negative self-talk, and to counter them with the tools learned in treatment. Finally, encourage your client to continue with the relaxation exercises as a good coping skill.

It's often good to schedule a 1-month follow-up session, or if preferable, a telephone review. Finally, encourage the client to contact you if he or she has further difficulty, and to return for booster sessions, if necessary.

Chapter 12 *Special Considerations*

This chapter addresses several special considerations that frequently arise in the course of treating people with PTSD who have been in an MVA. Selected topics include the following:

- Working with children

- Applying CBT in a group setting

- Physical pain and medical concerns that affect psychological treatment

- PTSD after a fatal accident

- The effect of lawsuits and the legal system on treatment

Children

Children require several special considerations.

First, PTSD presents somewhat differently in children, and you will need to keep this in mind. If you plan to use assessment instruments, you may need to contact the National Center for PTSD and review their recommendations for psychometric assessment and the use of special instruments.

Second, children must be approached differently, based on their psychological and cognitive development.

Third, children are minors, and you will need to obtain the consent of their parents to work with them, as well as the assent of the child in pursuing treatment. Parents and guardians will have some involvement in treatment, and they also exert considerable influence over the child's life.

This will include how they respond to the child's distress. The child should also agree to enter the treatment.

Despite these challenges, a growing body of empirical literature supports the use of CBT with children (e.g., Yule, 1999).

Groups

There have been several attempts to work with MVA survivors in groups. This approach can cause considerable challenges, such as how to present CBT skills in a way that accommodates the pace of change and the therapeutic involvement of each group member, the individual needs of each client, and the time it takes to address each person's issues while moving in a directed fashion.

In situations such as a train crash or a bus accident, groups of people may be injured at the same time and may benefit from CBT conducted in a group setting. In this situation, the group leader or leaders should be very experienced and must be comfortable with both providing CBT and working with a group. There is little empirical research to guide treatment, but this approach would seem to make considerable clinical sense if the events merited it (Young & Blake, 1999).

Pain and Ongoing Medical Issues

We have had considerable experience in working with clients who suffered physical injury in an MVA that left them in ongoing pain. Important clinical concerns include:

- Pain as a constant reminder of the MVA

- Limitations in physical functioning that lead to anger and frustration as a result of the MVA

- A desire to focus on physical injury as a way to avoid the psychological symptoms

- The use of medications that affect the client's mental state

In our research, we were very aware that we had limited time to address each client's psychological symptoms. As a result, we limited treatment specifically to the symptoms of PTSD that followed an MVA. We did not minimize the impact of their physical injury, but rather focused on the purpose of why they had come to us, which was to deal with their psychological symptoms.

In clinical practice, it is rarely possible to keep as clean a division of physical and psychological symptoms. In clinical practice, one could use cognitive techniques for the treatment of pain as they make sense, such as CBT, hypnosis, and supportive treatments. Some therapists feel comfortable taking on this component of treatment, and others do not. Each therapist must decide whether his or her orientation and experience are compatible with this type of treatment. If the therapist does not feel confident working in this area, then our experience suggests that referring these individuals for this care by specialists would not interfere with treatment outcomes, and in fact may be helpful in keeping the focus of treatment on the psychological treatments, as well as limiting the time of CBT intervention.

Death

In our experience, survivors of MVAs in which someone died face especially difficult psychological problems. The survivors may experience the loss of a loved one, may feel a sense of responsibility for the death, and may even have a loss of memory about the event, which makes the traumatic loss even more difficult to deal with directly.

Treatment will need to address the themes of loss and possible guilt and responsibility for the loss and also allow the necessary time and flexibility to address these issues therapeutically as part of the ongoing treatment. Some MVA survivors may have intrusive thoughts and memories related to loss and guild. These thoughts can be addressed with CBT, but more traditional treatments may also be warranted and helpful. The therapist's personal qualities should not be underestimated, and as noted in the early CBT literature, they have always been a critical variable in therapeutic success.

In many cases, a therapist who is treating a client who has been involved in a serious MVA will be working with lawyers and the legal system. It is important that the therapist feel comfortable in this environment.

Before they begin to treat MVA survivors, therapists should recognize the demands of working with this population. These include the need to share treatment notes and evaluations with insurance companies and lawyers. In addition, in many states, therapists may have the treatment that they provide scrutinized and assessed by independent medical examiners who are paid by defense attorneys or insurance companies.

The legal system has been criticized for negatively impacting some clients (e.g., Rogers, 1997). Several prominent PTSD researchers have noted that the need for depositions, the experience of meeting with attorneys, and the generally adversarial legal process can bring about a secondary traumatization in some victims of MVAs. It is important to help clients to prepare for these events and to apply the tools used in treatment to manage the stress of these events as well as possible.

Overall, the tools used in this comprehensive, flexible approach to treating victims of MVAs have held up very well to the wide variety of special needs that arise. The creativity of the therapist, in combination with the empirically derived treatments, should be applied as experience and current treatment guidelines support.

References

Alexander, D. (1999). The presentation of adult symptoms. In E. J. Hickling & E. B. Blanchard (Eds.), *International handbook of road traffic accidents & psychological trauma: Current understanding, treatment & law* (pp. 1–14). Amsterdam: Elsevier.

American Psychiatric Association. (1994). *Diagnostic and statistical manual of mental disorders* (4th ed.). Washington, DC: Author.

Beck, A. T., Rush, A. J., Shaw, B. F., & Emery, G. (1979) *Cognitive therapy of depression.* New York: Guilford Press.

Blanchard, E. B., & Hickling, E. J. (1997). *After the crash: Assessment and treatment of motor vehicle accident survivors.* Washington, DC: American Psychological Association.

Blanchard, E. B., & Hickling, E. J. (2004). *After the crash: Assessment and treatment of motor vehicle accident survivors* (2nd ed.). Washington, DC: American Psychological Association.

Blanchard, E. B., Hickling, E. B., Barton, K. A., Taylor, A. E., Loos, W. R., & Jones-Alexander, J. (1996). One-year prospective follow-up of motor vehicle accident victims. *Behaviour Research and Therapy, 34,* 775–786.

Blanchard, E. B., Hickling, E. J., Devineni, T., Veazey, C. H., Galovski, T. E., Mundy, E., et al. (2003). A controlled evaluation of cognitive-behavioral therapy for posttraumatic stress in motor vehicle accident survivors. *Behaviour Research and Therapy, 41,* 79–96.

Blanchard, E. B., Hickling, E. J., Freidenberg, B. M., Malta, L. S., Kuhn, E., & Sykes, M. A. (2004). Two studies of psychiatric morbidity among motor vehicle accident survivors one year after the crash. *Behaviour Research and Therapy, 42,* 569–583.

Blanchard, E. B., Hickling, E. J., Mitnick, N., Taylor, A. E., Loos, W. R., & Buckley, T. C. (1995). The impact of severity of physical injury and perception of life threat in the development of post-traumatic stress disorder in motor vehicle accident victims. *Journal of Traumatic Stress, 11,* 337–354.

Blanchard, E. B., Hickling, E. J., Taylor, A. E., Loos, W. R., & Forneris, C. A. (1996). Who develops PTSD from motor vehicle accidents? *Behaviour Research and Therapy, 34,* 1–10.

Breslau, N., Davis, G. C., Andreski, P., & Peterson, E. (1991). Traumatic events and post-traumatic stress disorder in an urban population of young adults. *Archives of General Psychiatry, 48,* 216–222.

Bryant, R. A., & Harvey, A. G. (2000). *Acute stress disorder: A handbook of theory, assessment and treatment.* Washington, DC: American Psychological Association Books.

Bryant, R. A., Harvey, A. G., Dang, S. T., Sackville, T., & Basten, C. (1998). Treatment of acute stress disorder: A comparison of cognitive-behavioral therapy and supportive counseling. *Journal of Consulting and Clinical Psychology, 66,* 862–866.

Bryant, R. A., Moulds, M. L., & Gutherie, R. M. (2000). Acute stress disorder scale: A self-report measure of acute stress disorder. *Psychological Assessment, 12,* 61–68.

Bryant, R. A., Sackville, T., Dang, S. T., Moulds, M., & Guthrie, R. (1999). Treating acute stress disorder: An evaluation of cognitive behavior therapy and supportive counseling techniques. *American Journal of Psychiatry, 156,* 1780–1786.

Buckley, T. C., Blanchard, E. B., & Hickling, E. J. (1996). A prospective examination of delayed onset PTSD secondary to motor vehicle accidents. *Journal of Abnormal Psychology, 105,* 617–625.

Ehlers, A., Mayou, R. A., & Bryant, B. (1998). Psychological predictors of chronic posttraumatic stress disorder after motor vehicle accidents. *Journal of Abnormal Psychology, 107,* 508–519.

Ellis, A. (1962). *Reason and emotion in psychotherapy.* New York: Lyle Stuart.

Fein, M. L. (1993). *I. A. M. (Integrated anger management): A common sense guide to coping with anger.* Westport, CT: Praeger.

Harvey, A. G., & Bryant, A. G. (1998). The relationship between acute stress disorder and posttraumatic stress disorder: A prospective evaluation of motor vehicle accident survivors. *Journal of Consulting and Clinical Psychology, 66,* 507–512.

Hickling, E. J., & Blanchard, E. B. (1992). Post-traumatic stress disorder and motor vehicle accidents. *Journal of Anxiety Disorders, 6,* 283–304.

Hickling, E. J., & Blanchard, E. B. (1997). The private practice psychologist and manual-based treatment: A case study in the treatment of posttraumatic stress disorder secondary to motor vehicle accidents. *Behaviour Research and Therapy, 35,* 191–203.

Hickling, E. J., & Blanchard, E. B. (Eds.). (1999). *International handbook of road traffic accidents and psychological trauma: Current understanding, treatment, and law.* New York: Elsevier.

Hickling, E. J., Blanchard, E. B., Buckley, T. C., & Taylor, A. E. (1999). Effects of attribution of responsibility for motor vehicle accidents on severity of PTSD symptoms. *Journal of Traumatic Stress, 12*(2), 345–353.

Hickling, E. J., Sison, G. F. P., & Vanderploeg, K. D. (1986). The treatment of posttraumatic stress disorder with biofeedback and relaxation training. *Biofeedback and Self-Regulation, 11,* 125–134.

Keane, T. M., Zimering, R. T., & Caddell, J. M. (1985). A behavioral formulation of post-traumatic stress disorder. *Behavior Therapist, 8,* 9–12.

Kessler, R. C., Sonnega, A., Bromet, E., Hughes, M., & Nelson, C. B. (1995). Post-traumatic stress disorder in the national Comorbidity Survey. *Archives of General Psychiatry, 52,* 1048–1060.

Mayou, R., Ehlers, A., & Bryant, R. (2002). Posttraumatic stress disorder after motor vehicle accidents: 3 year follow-up of a prospective longitudinal study. *Behaviour Research and Therapy, 40,* 665–675.

McKay, M., Rogers, P. D., & McKay, J. (1989). *When anger hurts: Quieting the storm within.* Oakland, CA: New Harbinger.

Meichenbaum, D. (1985). *Stress innoculation training.* New York: Pergamon Press.

Mowrer, O. H. (1947). On the dual nature of learning: The reinterpretation of "conditioning" and "problem solving." *Harvard Educational Review, 17,* 102–148.

Novaco, R. W. (1975). *Anger control: The development and evaluation of an experimental treatment.* Lexington, MA: Lexington Books.

Poppen, R. (1988). *Behavioral relaxation training and assessment.* Elmsford, NY: Pergamon Press.

Radloff, L. S. (1977). The CES-D scale: A self-report depression scale for research in the general population. *Applied Psychological Measurement, 1,* 385–401.

Rogers, R. (Ed.). (1997). *Clinical assessment of malingering and deception.* New York: Guilford.

U.S. National Highway Traffic Safety Administration. (2001, December). *Traffic safety facts 2000: A compilation of motor vehicle crash data from the fatal accident reporting system and general estimates system* (DOT HS 809 337). Washington, DC: Author.

U.S. National Highway Traffic Safety Administration. *2004 annual assessment: Crash fatality counts and injury estimates* [Data file]. Available from National Highway Traffic Safety Administration Web site, www.transportation.gov

Weathers, F., Litz, B. T., Herman, D. S., Huska, J. A., & Keane, T. M. (1993). *The PTSD checklist: Reliability, validity & diagnostic utility.* Paper presented at the annual meeting of the International Society for Traumatic Stress Studies, San Antonio, TX.

Wolpe, J. (1962). Isolation of a conditioning procedure as the crucial psycho-therapeutic factor: A case study. *Journal of Nervous and Mental Disease, 134,* 316–329.

Young, B. H., & Blake, D. D. (Eds.). (1999). *Group treatments for post-traumatic stress disorder.* Philadelphia: Brunner/Mazec.

Yule, W. (1999). Treatment of PTSD in children following road traffic accidents. In E. J. Hickling & E. B. Blanchard (Eds.), *The international handbook of road traffic accidents and psychological trauma: Current understanding, treatment, and law.* New York: Elsevier.

About the Authors

Edward J. Hickling, PsyD, received his doctorate in clinical psychology from the University of Denver, School of Professional Psychology, in 1982. He worked as the Director of Training and as a consultation liaison psychologist at the Veteran's Administration Medical Center in Albany, New York, until 1987, when he left to enter full-time private practice. In addition to his practice in clinical psychology, he holds positions as an adjunct professor at the State University of New York, Albany, in the Psychology Department, and is on the clinical faculty at the Albany Medical College, Department of Psychiatry. He has collaborated with Edward Blanchard and has held the position of Senior Research Scientist at the Center for Stress and Anxiety Disorders since 1990, when he became the Co-Principal Investigator with Blanchard on the first of several National Institute of Mental Health–funded grants investigating the psychological impact of motor vehicle accidents. Hickling has published more than 70 papers and several books, including two co-authored with Edward Blanchard on their work with motor vehicle accident survivors, *After the Crash: Assessment and Treatment of Motor Vehicle Accident Survivors,* and the edited volume, *International Handbook of Road Traffic Accidents and Psychological Trauma: Current Understanding, Treatment, and Law.* Current interests include innovative treatments (very brief therapy and online applications) for posttraumatic stress disorder, behavioral medicine, and psychological interventions in integrative and complementary medicine.

Edward B. Blanchard, PhD, ABPP, received his doctoral degree in clinical psychology from Stanford University in 1969. After brief stints at the University of Georgia (1969–1971), the University of Mississippi Medical Center (1971–1975), and the University of Tennessee Center for the Health Sciences in Memphis (1975–1977), he came to the University of Albany in 1977 as Professor and Director of Clinical Training. He was named Distinguished Professor of Psychology in 1989. In 2004, he retired and became Distinguished Professor Emeritus of Psychology. He has held National Institutes of Health grants in assessment and cognitive-behavioral treatments for headache, hypertension, and irritable bowel syndrome. His work on posttraumatic stress disorder began in the early 1980s, with an initial focus on Vietnam War veterans. Since 1989, he has collaborated with Edward Hickling on research on survivors of serious motor vehicle accidents. His work on this topic was supported by grants from the National Institute of Mental Health and forms the background for this book.